CULTURAL SHIFTING

Community
Leadership and Change

Al Condeluci

Training Resource Network, Inc. ▲ St. Augustine, Florida

First Edition

This publication is sold with the understanding that the publisher is not engaged in rendering legal, financial, medical, or other such services. If legal advice or other such expert assistance is required, a competent professional in the appropriate field should be sought. All brand and product names are trademarks or registered trademarks of their respective companies.

Published by Training Resource Network, Inc., PO Box 439, St. Augustine, FL 32085-0439. You may order direct from the publisher for $24.95 plus $3.00 shipping by calling 800-280-7010 or visiting our website at www.trninc.com.

Copy Editing: Beth Mansbridge, Dale DiLeo and Dawn Langton
Printed in the United States of America by Sheridan Books on acid-free paper.

Library of Congress Cataloging-in-Publication Data
Condeluci, Al.
    Cultural shifting : community, leadership, and change / Al Condeluci.--1st ed.
        p. cm.
    Includes bibliographical references and index.
    ISBN 1-883302-47-1 (alk. paper)
        1. Community organization. 2. Change. 3. Leadership. 4. Human services. I. Title

HM766.C66 2002
307--dc21

                                                                                    2002070004

CONTENTS

THE GREAT PEOPLE OF CULTURE ARE THOSE WHO HAD A PASSION FOR DIF-
FUSING, MAKING PREVAIL, FOR CARRYING FROM ONE END OF SOCIETY TO
THE OTHER, THE BEST IDEAS OF THEIR TIME.

— MATTHEW ARNOLD

ACKNOWLEDGMENTS

There are many people to thank and acknowledge during my journey completing this book. Since this book is the third in a trilogy, I refer you to the acknowledgment sections of the first two books, *Interdependence: The Route to Community* and *Beyond Difference*. All of these people need to continue to be thanked, but for this work, let me single out several key people.

First there is Training Resource Network. Dale DiLeo is an amazing man and I appreciate his confidence and trust in me. Although I knew of Dale and his incredible work around the country on behalf of full community life for people with disabilities, I finally got to meet and work with him in 1998 at a program in San Antonio, TX. His passion and intensity were intoxicating and there, at a San Antonio Spurs game in the Alamodome, we laid the blueprint for this book. All through the process, Dale was supportive and flexible and I thank him for his advice, counsel and support.

Next there is the UCP of Pittsburgh service system. In fact, the publication of *Cultural Shifting* marks my twenty-eighth year at this remarkable agency. Where else can one find such a supportive community that believes in the essence of inclusion of all people and practices it every day? To all the stakeholders at UCP, but especially Paul Dick, Patty Costantini, Shirlee Porro, Mary Buckholtz, Melva Gooden-Ledbetter, Lucy Spruill, Darla Lynn, Joyce Redmerski and Dan Rossi, I offer humble thanks. A special salute to Edie Scales, who has offered secretarial support to all three of my books.

Finally, there is my family. I suspect that if you have read any of the other items I have written you know something of my family. I talk about my extended and nuclear family at every chance I get. Family is such a critical part of who I am that to not include them here would be the greatest of omissions. I wish I could recognize all 125 members of the Condeluci family, but brevity would dictate that I focus in. So, to my wife, Liz, and children, Dante, Gianna and Santino, I offer this simple thanks. I know it does not make up for my many days away, but your presence with me, whether here or there, means more to me than you know.

And to all of my friends who have been with me in the course of change, thanks for the ideas, challenge and inspiration that the process offers. *Cultural Shifting* is about this process of change–so, let the change begin!

Al Condeluci
McKees Rocks, PA
March 2002

PREFACE
On Change and Leadership

All of us have thought about change. Some have done deep analytical thinking. Others have been called to promote change at work, school or an association to which we might belong. Still others have had an agonizing experience that has forced change. Change: It is something we all are called to do. Yet many have difficulty with it, or avoid it altogether. Change creates an inevitable reality in all of our lives, yet we seek to hold on to that which we know.

And leadership change–though many may not perceive themselves to be leaders–inspires leadership. If you are challenged to change, then a new part of you must emerge to meet the change and bring it forward. In some analysis, if you do not have change tapping at the door, leaders are less likely to emerge. Thus change and leadership are allied. Leaders promote change and change brings out the leader in us.

In my years of community experience, I have had an intimate dance with change and leadership. I have been asked to lead change for certain things in my community, or at my church or at my agency. I have been asked to talk at conferences or other educational gatherings about change and leadership. I have taught graduate school classes on change and leadership. I have watched change occur and leaders struggle to address it. I have witnessed some people bring about extraordinary change, and I have winced as smart people have bungled change opportunities.

Both change and leadership are elusive subjects that have relevance to everyone. They have significance in our private lives as we think about things we need to change, or consider what must be addressed that will result in change. With our interpersonal circles, we also have opportunities to change. We seek to change our children's behavior, or we try to change our spouse or we make that New Year's resolution to change our own behavior. In our associational lives, we look to change situations that exist in our church, neighborhood, PTA or bridge club. And finally, in our public roles, or places of employment, often we are asked to participate in or lead change for the good of the organization.

Yet change is one of those enigmas. Just when we think we have it figured out, something changes and we find we never really understood it in the first place. It is a concept that can be explored, even academically analyzed, but there isn't one of us who is truly an expert when it comes to applying change principles. Change is a perplexing phenomenon that warrants more attention, but even with deep focus and the best of processes, it can escape our grasp.

Leadership too, is equally challenging. What makes a leader? Are some people natural born leaders, or do challenging situations bring out the leader in any of us? Can we become better leaders? These are also issues that are elusive. Many have written about change and leadership, but still we struggle.

In the spirit of perseverance, however, I am taking another look at change and leadership. Using a process that seems to make sense to me, I want to invite you to consider change one more time. I have taken both an analytic as well as practical approach with ideas and examples of how change has, or hasn't, worked in personal, interpersonal and public efforts.

This book looks at change and leadership through the lens of culture and community. By considering the elements of culture and community it deals with personal, professional, organizational and cultural change. It explores the frameworks that surround change and attempts to dissect this concept by framing the aspects of community. It anchors around some of the most accepted theories on change and leadership, but it is not predicated on academic actions. Rather it uses more conventional wisdom and an anthropological spirit of the streets. Woven with stories and anecdotes, the nature of culture, community, the process of change and leadership and our resistance to the change process are explored. From the great philosophers to the person on the street, we will look at the notions of change and leadership and attempt to weave strategies to bring us to the cusp of managing change.

So, if you have picked up this book to address some personal directions, if you manage an organization needing to change, if you are looking to lead or change a group or mobilize a constituency, if a friend recommended you review it or if you have heard me present at a conference, I hope this book will have something you can use.

Chapter 1 is titled "Wanting More" and it considers the paradox between keeping the status quo and striving to get more. The notions of fear of change, coupled with the desire for more, create a real tension that can immobilize. Yet both of these things–fear and seduction, are the starting points for understanding change.

The second chapter, "Culture and Community," sets the structure for the notion of change and introduces the elements of community and the concept of "social capital." We look at recent evidence that community is on a decline as more and more people join less and less in community. This, in turn, has put our connectedness and social capital at risk. By understanding the basic elements of community and how people create culture, we gain a start point for promoting community and enhancing the resurgence of social capital.

In the third chapter, "Principles of Cultural Shifting," the main thesis for this book emerges. As cultures begin to add new people, products or ideas, a shift begins. This shift is the genesis for change. Once the culture begins to embrace a new way to do its business, an uncanny ability to elasticize emerges within the community. Using the concept of the "gatekeeper," these new people, products and ideas get their start point in shifting the culture. In essence, the gatekeeper is the critical element to change.

Chapter 4, "The Challenges of Change," introduces the reader to the structure and flow of change. This review includes looking at the types, zones, roles and resistances that are associated with the change process. In addition, it explores the critical elements of vision and change.

Chapter 5, "Framework for Change" offers an analysis of the change process seen through a number of differing lenses. By exploring these successful change paradigms, the chapter introduces a dynamic cultural change framework.

The sixth chapter, "Cultural Leadership," moves the reader toward not only the notions of leadership, but also to how the successful change agent utilizes the elements of culture and community to promote change. All of us, regardless of station, are called upon to lead and this chapter establishes how a leadership framework, thinking and communications can be embraced for cultural shifting.

The final chapter is titled "Strategies for Cultural Shifting" and offers some direct ideas and suggestions for applying the principles of cultural shifting in your work or life. Using examples, this chapter attempts to personify the notion of cultural shifting. The book concludes with a short "Epilogue."

▲

Yes, change is a phenomenon that is simple, yet complex. It taxes us by creating fear, yet can bring about amazing energy. It can sadden and inspire us at the same time. It is a topic we must embrace, for change is ever present.

Change is nothing more than a flow of new ideas, products or people into the culture. As the new ideas penetrate the community, a shift from the original focus gives way to a new approach. This shift from one element of culture to another offers us a ledgehold in which we can understand, and then manage the change process.

So sit back and dig into *Cultural Shifting*. The broader cultural concepts offer a framework not only to think about change, but to manage it as well.

IF WE ARE TO ACHIEVE A RICHER CULTURE, RICH IN CONTRASTING VALUES, WE MUST RECOGNIZE THE WHOLE GAMUT OF HUMAN POTENTIALITIES, AND SO WEAVE A LESS ARBITRARY SOCIAL FABRIC, ONE IN WHICH EACH DIVERSE HUMAN GIFT WILL FIND A FITTING PLACE.

— MARGARET MEAD

THE GREAT LAW OF CULTURE IS, LET EACH BECOME ALL THAT HE WAS CRE-
ATED CAPABLE OF BEING.

— THOMAS CARLYLE

FOREWORD
Cultural Shifting: Closing the Gap Between Ideals and the Law

ILISE L. FEITSHANS

One of the most striking aspects of Al Condeluci's discussion of cultural shifting is his facile manner of bringing together discordant threads of social and political theories into a whole cloth—reweaving the fabric of our society into a comforter of interdependence that can warmly surround our otherwise fragmented and fragile social structure.

Inclusion is necessary for society to survive. Gently, but firmly, this book makes it very clear that people within society need each other. But this book goes further to make the salient point that the ability of society to survive is linked to the flourishing of communities where each member of society has dignity because they are appreciated. And that attitudes in society about the useful and essential contributions of each individual, regardless of ability or disability, are shaped in part by our collective understanding about need, also called interdependence.

The social fabric woven of interdependence is a whole cloth—not only does it embrace every member of the community, but it also includes the contributions of every member of society. Inclusion, as the term is called under laws in the United States, means bringing people who were formerly hidden or invisible in institutions or edged away from collective consciousness into the mainstream of society. This is required to occur in public education, in employment and in public accommodations by law. This includes the Americans with Disabilities Act (ADA), one of the most beautifully written and artfully crafted laws in U.S. congressional legislative history. It also includes laws like the Rehabilitation Act and the Individuals with Disabilities Education Act (IDEA) and a host of other human relations laws that are implemented by states, the federal government and local human rights commissions.

But is writing and passing federal law enough of an act of collective will to operationalize the necessary social change? When laws cannot answer the needs of the people, when they can no longer embrace the people they protect within the social fabric, they become useless and arcane. It becomes an obstacle to true human relations. And, inevitably, it can be changed.

Ironically, it is not the law that has become a remnant of the past in the area of disability rights. The shroud of stigma has been cast off by the law long ago. Over three decades of progressive legislative changes in the way in which disability is defined and supported in the U.S., culminated in 1990 with the passage of the ADA.

Inclusion is the key to successful interdependence. Exclusion is the death of society, the end of community that thrives through interdependence. Yet so many people are afraid to step out of themselves and embrace a disaffected population. To achieve the goals codified in our laws, there must be a process, called here "cultural shifting." Yet, in truth, the detailed analysis set forth here about rituals and jargon and cultural patterns that need to change is really summarized in one word: implementation.

The rules and regulations that mandate inclusion changed a set of painfully antiquated inequities in our society with the stroke of the legislative pen. That was over a decade ago. But the law was leading, not codifying the social change. The law was written prospectively, to bring society back to a place of interdependence, where community would accept people with disabilities.

That has not yet happened fully in real life, even though those ideals are in fact already a part of the rituals of our society under law. In the paradigm described here, institutionalization of people with disabilities will soon be a bad collective memory, just as the history of having people's needs ignored and overlooking their abilities is no longer acceptable under law.

We must seek out ways for people with disabilities to fully participate in our society, because people with disabilities, when unshackled from the burdens of stigma and prejudice and the soft bigotry of low expectations, can contribute to our society.

We do not need new laws to achieve these goals. We do not even need more revisions or amplifications or modifications of the existing laws.

We need to change our cultural values, to engage in "cultural shifting" in our daily practices regarding people with disabilities and other disaffected populations, in order to bring our society into compliance with our existing, beautifully crafted antidiscrimination laws that protect those people who are "regarded as impaired" under the ADA.

In sum, another name for implementation is really "cultural shifting," or fixing the damage by doing the hard work of changing the realities of society.

That is really what this book is about: erasing the bad collective memory of wrongful treatment of people with disabilities, and replacing it with a healthy, interdependent framework for community. A new vision of society was written with the legislative pen. Now, the writing is over. Let the process of cultural shifting begin.

I.L. Feitshans, JD anScM
Adjunct Faculty, Cornell University
107 Centre St., Haddonfield, NJ 08033
ilise@prodigy.net

INTRODUCTION

The notion of cultural shifting is always tied to changes and adjustments of a community to something new or different. As we will explore in this work, when a gatekeeper of a community introduces a new person, idea or product, the current members have one of three options. They can embrace the new thing and incorporate it into the fold. They can reject it outright and work to keep it from penetrating into the community. Lastly, they can just ignore or disregard it as not being applicable to their interests.

Back in 1990, when I was writing *Interdependence: The Route to Community*, I attempted to introduce to the human service community a different way of viewing people who had a difference. Rather than think about fixing or changing things that are considered different, I proposed we look at finding ways these different things could fit in as they are. This was the beginning of a trilogy.

Next came the book *Beyond Difference* in 1996. This effort further explored how difference is perceived in our culture and took an inward turn to examine personal perspectives related to difference. The book suggested there are five critical variables necessary for individuals to get beyond the barriers often imposed by difference. These variables are simple, personal ones that must be in place if the culture wants to be inclusive.

Now the last of the trilogy, *Cultural Shifting*, introduces a macroscopic exploration of incorporating difference into community. This book was designed to identify the broader cultural variables essential in the change process. If we understand how a community can incorporate new things, the realities of inclusion can come alive.

"TAKE SOME MORE TEA," THE MARCH HARE SAID TO ALICE, VERY EAR-
NESTLY. "I'VE HAD NOTHING YET," ALICE REPLIED IN AN OFFENDED
TONE, "SO I CAN'T TAKE MORE." "YOU MEAN YOU CAN'T TAKE LESS,"
SAID THE HATTER, "IT'S VERY EASY TO TAKE MORE THAN NOTHING."
— LEWIS CARROLL

CHAPTER 1
Wanting More

Every type of business, from technology to human services, can analyze its out-comes and successes between of its status quo and its drive to find new ways to improve. The status quo is the way things are typically done, the ongoing frame-work of services or products. The drive to improve is pushed by internal energy to get better and external competition that someone else might pass you by. This constant struggle between that which we find comfortable and that which can be better creates a zone of tension for leaders as they attempt to manage organizations today.

In my own field of human services and supports to people with disabilities, the same challenge is in play. This field evolved from professionals taking care of vul-nerable people to supporting these same people in becoming independent. More recently, the field has continued to advance to the current concepts of interdepen-dence, self-determination and consumer control. These "buzzwords" suggest that people with disabilities can and should be connected and supported to develop their own relationships within a community.

An analysis of this goal, however, is disturbing when we look at the reality of disability in our society today. Data show that people with disabilities, more than any other minority group, are isolated and set apart from the greater society (Har-ris, 1998). From housing to transportation to jobs, people with disabilities are well behind the norm.

Traditional approaches to addressing these shortcomings just have not gleaned the results that people with disabilities and their allies have wanted (Condeluci, 1991). But, by using a cultural perspective, perhaps we can offer another approach to community inclusion. First, let's examine some of the problems in this area.

Continued Segregation

A key area that must change is the continued segregation of vulnerable people. Historically, the phenomenon of segregation has been a way that societies have

3

positioned people perceived to be different from one another. Ethnic, religious, socioeconomic and age differences are but a few reasons why people have drawn lines. In some cases the segregation has been self-imposed or sought out by the group, but more often than not the polarizations have been relegated. A dominant group has decided who is welcomed and who is not. Examples of this cultural distancing can be observed around the globe today and over time, but perhaps the most penetrating example is the Holocaust.

Recently I visited the U.S. Holocaust Museum in Washington, DC, where the profound effects of congregation, segregation and then elimination are graphically portrayed. At this time (and many might argue for years before and since), the effects of anti-Semitism were deeply etched. Using the classic lines of religious and cultural differences, Jews were initially banned and banished from the majority Aryan society. As hatred and misunderstanding (as the distancing of peoples can cause) grew, the dominant society began to deepen its polarization until the ultimate destruction was launched.

When people are segregated from each other, myths and misunderstanding will abound. The differences will be accentuated and each group will feel increasingly irrelevant to each other. Usually this will lead to a deep deterioration that results in negative behavior. This has happened over and over.

Medical Treatment Approach for People with Disabilities

Overall, the congregation and segregation of people with disabilities has been medically recommended and, in a way, sanctioned by society. When people with disabilities are referred to a program or separate setting, it is often because the dominant group feels this is a better setting for them to get help or treatment. This medical paradigm has been well documented as the prevailing approach to dealing with people who have disabilities. A classic notion of this prototype is the congregation of people perceived to be sick or deficient. This congregation was first initiated with hospitals and clinics, then facilities, institutions and state schools and hospitals. The final vestige of this type of congregation is found with nursing homes and hospices. All of these are offset facilities designed to "take care of" a particular population.

There are two powerful reasons why this type of congregation is so dominant, even to this day, for people with disabilities. The first reason is the prominence of medicine and agents of the medical model. Because they often deal with life-and-death situations, physicians usually are given a Godlike status in most cultures. When a physician makes a recommendation, it is usually respected and followed.

To underscore this point, there is an age-old tale about the physician who dies and upon reaching the gates of Heaven, is appalled by the long line to get in. Trying to pull rank, he sees a guardian angel tending the line and asks, as a physician, if there is any way he can jump the line and move closer to the front. The guardian angel says no, and the physician waits his turn in line for what seems to be hours. Just before he reaches the gate, a very angelic-looking man with a stethoscope and medical bag jumps the line and gets in front. Annoyed, the physician summons the guardian angel and says: "*What's the deal? I asked an hour ago if I could jump the line and you said no. Then up walks this other doctor and he gets right in the gate with no wait.*" The guardian angel replies: "*That's no doctor, it's just God – He likes to pretend He's a doctor.*"

This joke underscores the societal dominance of medical agents. When these people make a recommendation, most of us follow, often without question about the consequences. Add to this the economic and often physical devaluations that position people with disabilities as poor, inferior or inept, and the segregation and congregation rarely gets questioned. When people are perceived as weak or incapable, they fall prey to the opinion and recommendations of professionals. The net result is that everyone, professionals, the community and people with disabilities and their families, think that congregation and segregation are the best approach.

It is important to understand that in this context, the separation of people with disabilities from the greater society is not a mean-spirited or malicious activity. In most cases, everyone involved wants what is best. The notion of congregation and segregation as the best approach is what is at question.

Low Wages and Devaluation of Direct Support Staff

If a human or social services agency employs you, there are probably some unique aspects about you. For the most part you are driven by the notion of service. You have decided that you wanted to make your life count for some human betterment. As "Pollyannish" as it may seem, you have decided that justice and fairness for people is important and the employment choice you have made is probably tied to this agenda. Certainly you do not do this work for the money. We all know that human services workers are grossly underpaid. Still you stay and continue to attempt to address the specific aspect of your agency's mission. To this end you are particularly vulnerable.

This vulnerability is tied to three converging issues. One is that you are sincerely interested in the people you serve and their full participation in the community. If you work for a vocational agency you want to see people get jobs; if you work for a residential agency you want to see the residents safely involved and accepted in community; if you work for a poverty agency you want to see your clients have access to income. Yet the reality is that the challenges (as summarized earlier) remain, regardless of your hard work. For every person you help get a job, five more are waiting in your office. For every person involved in community, there are seven more at risk in community, and on and on. This struggle continues until you slowly begin to feel that anything you do will not really support people in meaningful ways.

Then, add this to the challenging schedules of this type of work and the number of hours you invest or ask your people to work. Most of us employed in human services know that the hours seem to never end. There is always another meeting to attend or proposal to write. There is always another shift to fill or person to call. These demands are pressing. Additionally, the ante gets upped when the work that is performed is vital. In my organization, if the staff is not on duty, then a person might not get up for the day. Or if a staff member does not show up, a crucial medicine might be missed, or a meal might not be rendered. These are not small issues; agencies are experiencing a rising number of abuse cases, as noted by news reports and lawsuits.

The final vulnerability for human services staff rests with salary. If there is one major problem that almost every human services organization I know faces, it is low salaries paid to their frontline workers. This challenge is evident around the United States and Canada and has resulted in pending "Living Wage Laws" being introduced and legislated. Indeed, in California, a lawsuit has been filed by community-based human services agencies, citing the wage disparity between state employees and community-based employees who do the same type of work.

The problem of low salaries is multifaceted. In the United States, as states began to shift services from direct state-run facilities to community services, contracts for care were established with many nonprofit organizations. Over the years, the allotted funds for these contracts have not kept up with rising state wage levels, resulting in a major disparity around the country between state employees and private contracted employees. In Pennsylvania, state employees on the front line providing services to the few people remaining in institutions are paid twice that of their agency counterparts in the community. This disparity must change.

Another reason for low salaries in human services is the devaluation of vulnerable people. Historically, people with disabilities, poor people, the elderly and children have been devalued in society and are at greater risk. This devaluation has manifested in a number of ways including physical/psychological abuse, institutionalization and premature mortality. Given this, people who have worked with or cared for these same vulnerable populations have been similarly devalued with low wages. Quite simply, the question begs to be asked: if vulnerable people are not seen as valuable by society, why should people who care for them be paid adequately? Remarkably, in my city of Pittsburgh, attendants who work at the Pittsburgh Zoo are paid more than our staff who support people with disabilities.

These three notions, those of limited successes, difficult work and hours and low wages can converge to take the wind out of the sails of people who work for human services agencies. The net result is a sense of resignation. This leads to high levels of turnover or burnout that make the noble work of human services challenging and, often times, thankless.

Understanding the Challenges of Cultural Change

There is no easy answer to these realities, but there are some things we can do. Let's start by examining the challenge of changing a culture that has resisted solving these issues. Human beings are creatures of the status quo. Once we establish a routine or approach, we find ways to anchor these approaches to create patterns and habits in our lives. Over and over we develop predictable ways to address elements in our everyday lives.

Yet, at the same time, all of us want something more or different, for ourselves and the people we serve. We look at our material possessions or achievements we have enjoyed and we reach for more. In spite of our accomplishments we are never really satisfied. We can measure this reality in many different dimensions. Certainly in a material sense, most of us seem to be looking for more material belongings in our lives. One new toy leads to another. We are not satisfied with what we have. In human services, we also are not satisfied with our services and the problems we face.

In our businesses or organizations we are always looking for a new approach, a more focused niche, or a better way than that of other groups we know. Every year there seems to be a new or improved way of thinking about business. We have had Theory X, Management by Objectives, Quality Circles, Chaos Leadership, Learning Organizations and the like. In human services we have had supported employment, supported living, circles of support and self-determination. Yet, in spite of these innovations, we still find that the outcomes lag.

Similarly, our personal lives with family and friends are always being adjusted and altered. Suggestions from consultants and experts challenge us to review the depth and quality of our relationships and community connections. Of course, this leads to a plethora of advice from all angles on how we can improve our friendships and intimate relationships. We want more.

Even in our spiritual lives we are called to reflect more, to pray more, to meditate and chant more, so we can improve and enhance our relationship with our God. Retreats and spiritual advisors have become commonplace as people enhance their quest for more. As the face of society continues to change, however, many people find themselves in different realities than they remember as children or may have wanted for themselves. The demographic shift in the family alone offers an interesting lens on differences for people. Most adults today were raised in a family constellation that is now very different for their own families.

This shift in culture has created for some a void with family. Rather than the large and more closely knit families of the past, today's families are smaller, single-parent-driven or dispersed around the country. Indeed, theorists have looked at the changing face of culture (Putnam, 2000) and have made an analysis of the decline of "social capital" or the connectedness between people in their communities. This notion of social capital is predicated on the fact that throughout the history of the United States, Americans developed deep associational roots that built social capital. The relationships that we developed were framed from a mutual sense that we are all in this together.

Alexis de Tocqueville first wrote about this concept of social connectedness in his 1850 analysis of the United States titled, *Democracy in America*. In this work, de Tocqueville described a phenomena he called "habits of the heart" where people watched out for each other for no other apparent reason than what is good for you is good for me. By the end of the Civil War and beyond the turn of the century in the 1900s, Americans began to enhance these "habits of the heart" to a whole new level. As our society shifted from primarily agrarian to industrial mode, and as immigrants came from all the Eastern European countries, all types of clubs, groups and associations began to develop and strengthen. From 1871 until 1920, over sixty groups moved from a parochial context to become nationwide entities, all creating a buildup of culture, community and connections. People need people, and need to feel useful.

The continued development of community occurred aggressively throughout the early 1900s and, according to Putnam, seemed to reach its peak in 1960. At this time clubs, leagues, trade associations, unions, fraternal groups and other types of amalgamations continued to build social capital and connectedness amongst people.

Since 1960, however, sociologists have begun to detect a decline in this energy to join and connect through clubs, groups and associations. This decline has had a profound effect on this notion of social capital and in turn has begun to reshape how people see each other and the community at large. For example, Putnam reports that twenty-five years ago, nearly two-thirds of people surveyed said they trusted other people. A similar survey today revealed this trust had slipped to where two-thirds now say they do not trust others. In 1970 most Americans entertained friends in their homes an average of fifteen times each year. Now, similar people report that they entertain only seven times per year. Further, by the mid-1970s, almost two-thirds of Americans regularly attended club meetings. Now, two-thirds never attend club or group meetings.

These data begin to suggest that when people spend less and less time together, it hastens the continued decline of community and the friendships it brings. Yet most of us crave to have all that we think is good in our society: family, friends, strong social and civic relationships.

This longing for more is not necessarily a bad thing. It pushes us to move forward, and as we improve we undoubtedly enhance society and life. Many of our improvements have increased the quality and impact of life in general. These improvements and changes are the hallmarks of culture; they are the results of wanting more.

Of course, this quest for improvement and ultimate perfection can create an equal sense of frustration. People who lag behind the latest trends, be they in business, life or spirit, can feel like they are not keeping up. These pressures can cause some to drop out, or to even stop trying. The notions that some are winners and ahead of the game and others are losers can create a divide in society. These perspectives can be damaging and often have a negative effect on society in general. When people feel they are failures, or that they are not able to achieve what they had hoped for, those around them can feel the ripples. People begin to lose confidence and social energy.

Still, the struggle to improve, to want more, seems to be a human dimension that cannot be stopped or altered. From the time we started observing and measuring culture, the march to advance, improve and find a better way has always won in the long run. New products and ideas continue to introduce better or more convenient ways for culture to improve. Often these ideas and products have enhanced the free time that people have to dream and then plan things that make society better. The influx of new people, too, continues to add to the depth of community.

As new people get incorporated into the culture, they cause others to redefine and enhance their structure and dimensions. These changes have the potential to help build community.

This march to improvement has a strong effect on people within the culture. As the pace, tempo and diversity increases, people have to make decisions on where they stand on all of this. The new products, people or ideas that become introduced to culture bring many good things, but they also bring stress and fears.

Sociologists who have looked at the penetration of new ideas or products (or people) into a culture call this "diffusion theory." Over the years these social scientists have analyzed the spread of these innovations into society. One 1930s study looked at how the emerging use of hybrid corn diffused amongst farmers. As the use of the new corn seed slowly diffused into the culture, the various phases and those who embraced the change were charted as follows:

Phase One: Innovators–This was the small group of players who introduced the new seeds.

Phase Two: Early Adopters–These were the opinion leaders in the community who began to adopt what the innovators had done.

Phase Three: Early Majority–This group, larger than the first two, stepped up and began to incorporate the new idea.

Phase Four: Late Majority–This next large group then adopted the idea after the first three groups had proven its viability.

Phase Five: Laggards–This was the final group who reluctantly found their way to the new idea.

In this schema, the Innovators and Early Adopters are the visionaries, the ones willing to take risks in promoting new ideas and products. They are the positive gatekeepers, a concept this book focuses on later. The flow, however, from one group to the next is not necessarily a smooth or easy one. Many a good idea or product never gets beyond the first two phases. This reality causes anthropologists to explore more closely how and why some ideas make it and others don't. Most critical to the flow is how the culture communicates and how ideas can translate from one group to the next.

As one considers this reality and how people in community position around them, three major camps emerge. Although this may be an oversimplification, I feel these are important anecdotal observations. Certainly, deeper analysis will find that people can move within and among these three camps depending on the situation, but in general the three groupings seem viable. These are:

1. *Those that embrace and encourage new things.*

   These are the people who are optimistic, take risks and think openly. These folks are often younger and tend to be more liberal in nature. They are natural risk takers who see change as opportunity. They are the people who are Innovators or Early Adopters.

2. *Those that resist and discourage new things.*

   Such individuals are often reactionary and closed. In many regards these people are satisfied with what they have and do not embrace innovation.

They are usually older and more set in their ways. Most of these people never even make it to the Laggard level.

3. *Those who are neutral.*

This group waits for the trendsetters either way and then follows the one that dominates. As neutral people, they delay opinion until they have a stronger sense of what will play out in the long haul. This group produces the Early and Late Majorities.

All three camps exist in the field in human services. The organization I work for has a focus on assisting people with disabilities to become active parts of their community. As we promote this mission and reach out to citizens in the community, I run into all three groups. Some community members are quick to understand diversity and embrace people with disabilities who have been excluded from their communities. Others are resistant to any change and are uncomfortable around disability. Lastly, there are those individuals who really do not care or have an opinion on the matter.

These three types of people will be examined later in this book when we look at the notion of the "gatekeepers" of culture. The concept of change and cultural shifting, the very basis of wanting more, is directly related to how these types of people blend together in community. And not just these groupings of people that you find in community, but the overall analysis of culture and members of culture provides a fluid map for change. If we want more, and I see no stop to this quest, then the understanding of culture and community is critical.

Further, the notions of culture and community and how these elements relate to change and improvement offer an exciting framework for consideration. The more we understand how community works, the easier it might be to get in front of the change and the process of cultural shifting. Or, if you are not interested in being in front of change but still have a vested interest, a cultural analysis can still be helpful. The more we understand the process of cultural shifting from one perspective to another, the more we can lead, influence or control change. Not just wanting more, but achieving more is a reality.

YOU NEVER KNOW WHAT IS ENOUGH UNLESS YOU KNOW WHAT IS MORE THAN ENOUGH.

— WILLIAM BLAKE

THE BEHAVIOR OF AN INDIVIDUAL IS DETERMINED NOT BY THEIR BACKGROUND, BUT BY THE CHARACTER OF THEIR ANCESTRY AND CULTURAL ENVIRONMENT.

— FRANZ BOAS

CHAPTER 2
Culture and Community

This chapter is an overview of culture and community. It has particular relevance to people with disabilities and their allies. Since medical and clinical approaches have not led the way to greater opportunities for community inclusion, then another approach must be considered. By utilizing concepts of culture, we can find strategies and approaches that have stood the test of time.

Community is a network of people who regularly come together for some common cause or celebration. A community is not necessarily geographic, although geography can define certain communities. To come to an understanding of community is to appreciate that community really is based on the relationships that form, not on the space. In fact, space can be an abstract notion when it comes to understanding community. Think about the global community created by the Internet. These communities are not bound by geography, but are relationships forged in cyberspace.

The term "community" is the blending of the prefix "com," which means "with," and the root word, "unity," which means togetherness and connectedness. The notion of being "with unity" is a good way to think about the concept of community. When people come together for the sake of a unified position or theme, you have community.

The term "culture" is analogous to community, but culture relates more to the behaviors manifested by the community. People bound together around a common cause create a community, but the minute they begin to establish behaviors around their common cause they develop a culture. In this way, culture is the learned and shared way that communities do particular things.

This basic approach to community and culture blend three key features. One is the fact that community is a network of people. Often these people may have great differences or even distances between them. They can be different in age, background, ethnicity, religion or many other ways, but in spite of their differences, their commonality or common cause pulls them together. The similarity of the common cause or celebration is the second key feature of community and the glue that creates the network. Regardless of who the members of the network are as people, their common cause overrides whatever differences they may have and creates a powerful connection. Finally, as the collection of people continues to meet and celebrate on a regular basis, they begin to frame behaviors and patterns and become a culture, the third key ingredient. These regular meetings bond the community members as they discover other ways that they are similar.

Again, these three key features are:
1. Diversity of membership
2. Commonality of celebration
3. Regularity of gathering

One of the most important facets of community is that it promotes a sense of social capital for the members who belong. Social capital, as defined in Chapter 1, refers to the connections and relationships that develop around community and the value these relationships hold for the members. Like physical capital (the tools used by communities, or human capital, or the people power brought to a situation), "social capital" is the value brought on by the relationships.

L. J. Hanifan first introduced the idea of social capital in 1916. He defined it as:

"those tangible substances that count for most in the daily lives of people: namely good will, fellowship, sympathy, and social intercourse among the individuals and families who make up a social unit… The individual is helpless socially, if left to himself… If he comes into contact with his neighbor, and they with other neighbors, there will be an accumulation of social capital, which may immediately satisfy his social needs and which may bear a social potentiality sufficient to the substantial improvement of living conditions in the whole community. The community as a whole will benefit by the cooperation of all its parts, while the individual will find in his associations the advantages of the help, the sympathy, and the fellowship of his neighbors."

More recently, Robert Putnam (2000) defined the concept of social capital as: *"referring to connections among individuals–social networks and the norms of reciprocity and trustworthiness that arise from them…[It] is closely related to…civic virtue…A society of many virtuous but isolated individuals is not necessarily rich in social capital."* (p. 19)

Other sociologists suggest that social capital is enhanced by social currency. This idea is how social fodder links people together. For example, a popular person who is the life of the party might be regularly included in activities. To this extent he is strong in social capital. His jokes and storytelling, the items that make him popular in the gathering, are the social currency he exchanges.

Think about the many communities with which you are involved. People who might be different from you in many ways surround you—your family, your work team, your church, or your clubs or associations—but the commonality of the community tends to override the differences you have and create a strong norm for connections. The exchange is based in social currency. Further, these relationships become helpful to you for social reasons. Sociologists call this helpfulness "social reciprocity."

Social capital is critical to a community because it:

- allows citizens to resolve collective problems more easily
- greases the wheels that allow communities to advance smoothly
- widens our awareness of the many ways we are linked
- lessens pugnaciousness, or the tendency to fight or be aggressive
- increases tolerance
- enhances psychological processes, and as a result, biological processes

This last point prompts Putnam (2000) to assert:

"If you belong to no groups, but decide to join one, you cut your risk of dying over the next year in half!"

The fact that social capital keeps us safe, sane and secure cannot be understated. Most of us tend to think that institutions or organizations are key to safety. Places like hospitals or systems like law enforcement are thought to keep us safe, but the bold truth is that these systems have never really succeeded in keeping us safe or healthy. Rather, it is the opportunity for relationships that community offers us as well as the building of social capital. Simply stated, your circles of support and the reciprocity they create are the most important element in your safety. In fact, it has been suggested that social isolation, or the opposite of social capital, is responsible for as many deaths per year as is attributed to smoking.

When we consider social capital for people with disabilities, we must recognize the void. We know that people with disabilities still are separated from the greater community and mostly involved in special programs or services designed for them. In these realities, the major outlet for social capital is found only within the borders of the special programs. To this extent then, the relationships that constitute the social capital of many people with disabilities are other people with disabilities. The narrowness of this reality leaves a significant void.

Consider the notion of reciprocity. The more you become connected with your community, the more people begin to watch out for each other. If one day a regular member of your group doesn't show up, a natural inclination would be to check up on them. This sense of group reciprocity is what leads to individual safety.

If the major social capital outlet for people with disabilities is other people with disabilities, then the reciprocity factor can become narrow. The more narrow the confines of reciprocity the less impact it offers.

Putnam's ideas of how social capital builds tolerance and lessens pugnaciousness also fit closely to the concept of cultural shifting. Anthropologists have found that for communities to get better, new and different ideas, people or products are necessary. Yet intolerant and angry communities are not as open or as ready to absorb new things. Consequently, cultural shifting is more difficult when communities remain narrow. Social capital helps build tolerance because the exposure to others challenges us to consider new things. This developing openness then has an effect on pugnaciousness. Simply put, if you become more exposed to difference, anger levels have a greater potential to go down.

This notion of social capital and the blending of similarity of interest with natural diversity of the members create unique phenomena for growth and development in both people and organizations. The drive to find, create or be more than we had before is magically transformed when it is blended with community. The reciprocity developed through social capital is helpful as well for either specific or general reasons.

Many current business leaders understand the notion of community. Most successful companies and organizations work to create a community sense among their employees. A company can be energized by the idea that people can bond around a mission statement and objective to find mutual success. The relationships that form a bond create opportunities for social reciprocity and build social capital. In fact, about any organization or work force, including families, can lead to a greater sense of bonding, focus and success. Quite simply, community is a universal concept that creates advancement not only in products and ideas, but for people as well.

Cultures and communities have many features, but one key ingredient is regularity. That is, for a community to be viable it must have some regular points of contact and connection. For a family community, this might be annual reunions or the celebration of holidays together. For a religious community, this would be weekly services and holy days for celebration. For organizations, this would be regular staff meetings or stakeholder gatherings. For clubs, groups or associations, regular meetings or gatherings formalize the group as a community.

Other features of community include the notions of consent, creativity and cooperation. Robert Nisbit (1972) suggested that community thrives on self-help and equal consent. He felt that people do not come together merely to be together, but to do something together that cannot be done in isolation. Others (Sussman, 1959) identified community for its sense of interdependence. McKnight (1988) described community as a collective association driven toward a common goal.

Indeed, if we think about communities that we know, they all work toward some identified goal. From teaching people new skills, to saving souls, to addressing a common problem, to launching a government, all of these ventures capture the power of community, and then, through their behavior, create a culture.

Functions of Community

Warren and Warren (1979), researchers who studied community, have defined community through an understanding of its functions, which are:

1. *As a Sociability Arena*–This is where members of the community are able to forge relationships and friendships through daily interaction. This sociability is driven by the proximity of the community members.
2. *As an Interpersonal Influence Center*–This is where members of the community offer ideas and advice to fellow members especially in times of problems or struggles.
3. *As Mutual Aid*–Often in times of emergencies or extreme challenge, members of the community are available to each other for aid.
4. *As an Organizational Base*–This is when most members of the community feel a kindred notion of commonality that leads to an organization or a unique banding together.

5. *As a Reference Group*–This function suggests an identification, often associated with pride, or some other unique bonding. This is easily detected when members of the community introduce themselves based on their commonality.

6. *As a Status Arena*–This final function allows members to gauge or parade their status through involvement with the community.

These functions offer a sense of purpose that communities serve. Some or all of these six functions come into play when people gather around things they hold in common. For most of us, regardless of focus, the main purpose for joining any community is to celebrate something we are interested in and to develop relationships.

Elements of Community

Key elements of community are found in all types of communities that exist, be they formal or informal. As we identify these aspects of community, think about how they fit or relate to the communities you know.

Common Theme

All communities rally around a common theme. This theme is the very essence of the community, the reason for its being. For families, it is the lineage or heritage–the background of their ancestors. For workers, it is the mission, vision or agenda of the organization. For religions, it is the theology and belief structure of the congregation. For clubs and groups, it is the focus point for why the club gathers in the first place. For any gathering, there is a reason. This is, or relates to, the common theme for the community. In fact, the common theme is the deepest essence of the community. Consider the commonality found in these examples:

Family

The most basic network of people bound by some common cause is the family. All of us start out life and learn the basics of culture through our family. Along with our nuclear family, many of us have a larger, extended family that includes all aspects of our genealogy. Most of us have a fair handle on our ancestry and nurture our understanding through photos, stories and family reunions. My own family enclave consists of some fifteen families, and we are reminded daily of our commonality.

Spirituality

Most sustaining nations are anchored by strong spiritual cultures within their midst. A spiritual culture is a network of people bound together by a common theology. These cultures are usually organized as congregations, parishes, mosques, temples or other such venues of worship. Religious cultures are rooted in spiritual rituals and activities that, over time, become deeply ingrained.

Work

Another network of people bound by some common cause is a work community. Most of us, at some time in our lives, serve as members of a company, organization or agency. In these roles, despite our differences in ethnicity, age, religion or experience, we are all similar as employees. Indeed, successful companies work hard to create a distinct "work culture" where members can enhance morale by being members of the team. Other types of work cultures are trade associations or professional groups that represent certain types of disciplines or skills.

Age

Another delineation that can bond people into a culture is age. In fact, with our educational system set up with age-specific groups, we are all habituated with our age peers. Later in this book we will look at various generations and how these cohorts of people, through common cultural experiences, come to embrace change.

Neighborhood

The common aspects and concerns of their neighbors often influence people who live in certain areas. People who live in close proximity are often caught up with appearance, crime, safety, children and other elements that bond them. Some neighborhoods develop safety patrols, escorts and other methods to make sure their fellow neighbors are not victimized. These types of neighborhood groups offer a classic example of a network of people bound by a common issue.

Ethnicity

Many people use ethnicity as a point of commonality. This bond is so powerful that, regardless of any other factor, if you hold ethnic origins with another person it can lead to an instant identification. I know that in my own situation, as an Italian, many people will approach me at workshops or speeches I do and tell me that they too are Italian. These deep roots have led to all types of fraternal organizations that continue to honor and carry out their ethnic traditions.

Sexuality or Sexual Orientation

With the advent of the women's movement in the '60s, we began to see the bonding of people based on their sex. Along with women's groups, men's collectives also began to develop to help men find the commonality of their experience. In addition to this are the gay and lesbian cultures. These groups help to offer broader implications of being gay.

Common Interest

This catchall category refers to those networks of people who bond around some common interest. This could be people interested in photography, tennis, poetry, politics, darts, food, dogs or countless other avocations that people find in common. The list is virtually endless, and you can safely bet that if there is something that you deeply love or enjoy, there is a group that gathers around that interest. When you meet someone who enjoys the same thing as you, no matter how different he or she may be, you have an immediate connection.

▲

This notion of commonality is the root issue for the gathering of people and primary element of culture. There are a myriad of ways community gathers. Not long ago I was visiting the Carnegie Museum of Natural History in Pittsburgh with my youngest son, Santino. As we made our way around the various exhibits, we came across a display of seashells. The display was outstanding, and Santino and I paused as we considered the various sizes and shapes of these marvelous items. In the last display case, however, I noticed a small sign that read: *"The Pittsburgh Seashell Society meets the first Wednesday of each week at Hemingway's Café. All seashell lovers welcome!"*

I stopped to consider for a moment a meeting of the Seashell Society. I wondered what these folks do. What also resonated was the mere fact that something like seashells can bring people together in community. Indeed, most anything that people can find passion about results in some type of formal or informal community that gathers their fellow aficionados.

Membership

The people who gather to celebrate around a theme are called members of the community. These are the individuals who show an interest or passion for the reason around the gathering. Membership can be either formal or informal, based upon the intent of the community. That is, for some official gatherings or settings that have a formal focus, members might have to buy their way in. An example is a health club or spa. The reason for gathering, or the theme, is physical fitness, but the members must apply and be accepted into the community. They might even need to have a membership card to prove they are members of the community. Other communities are informal in nature and just a love for the theme is a card to membership. An example here might be parents who gather at the playground every day with their children. Regardless, people who join together forge this notion of membership.

A good way to get a handle on cultural membership is to think about the various communities that you belong to. This starts with the family in which you were born to membership. Some people may choose not to be associated with their family. But they can never be fully removed. Sometimes individuals disown their families and sometimes their families disown them. Even being disowned, however, does not totally remove you from the history you share with your relatives.

Membership in a spiritual culture is often a formal experience. In some cases a person may be born into a family that belongs to a church or religion, and there is an expectation he or she will be raised within the community by the parents. In other cases, people may choose a religion or theology in which to participate and then petition or study their way into the group. Once membership is established, the person becomes a formal player. This would include such things as inclusion in the congregation yearbook, or being named in the bulletin or weekly newsletter.

As youngsters, people begin membership in a number of cultures. The first of these is usually formal educational venues, beginning with kindergarten or pre-school and then moving into regular grade school. Membership in these settings is often driven by age, family financial income or area of residence. Once the child gets registered and the family pays the fees or tuition, the child is considered an official member of the culture.

During the experience of grade and high school, children are introduced to a number of interest or avocational cultures. These might include little league, dance school, music programs, soccer, basketball leagues, chess clubs, Boy Scouts and Girl Scouts, YMCA, science clubs and so on. Many of us know this experience all too well.

After high school, individuals consider membership into colleges, universities, trade schools, military or work cultures. These are all formal experiences that re-quire doing research and then considering which setting would be best for you. Once this choice is made, the individual petitions to become a member, and might or might not be accepted. With college, for example, if a person does not have the grades or SAT scores to merit admission, a petition for membership, no matter how desired, would be rejected. Membership, be it formal or informal, is always a two-way street.

Young adults access other cultural venues, both formal and informal. Groups, gangs, clubs, associations or hobby groups are all examples of the potency of com-munity. As social animals, human beings want to belong or be considered a mem-ber. Even in an informal sense, the notion of membership and belonging is deeply embedded in our psyche.

The membership drive of belonging can best be understood through the con-cept of inclusion. In fact, inclusion is a word that is used in a number of areas. Elected officials talk often about the politics of inclusion. This is the notion that all people are welcome and needed in a democracy. When people are included, they belong to the political process.

The paradigm of human services also uses the concept of inclusion as a core ingredient. Here, social services workers talk about including people with disabili-ties or differences in the mainstream community. The entire notion of deinstitutionalization, or the moving out of institutionalized residents into com-munity-based services and supports, is driven by the goal of inclusion.

Inclusion is also a key element in civil rights. Discrimination is often seen as the opposite of inclusion. When people are discriminated against, they are not included into the mainstream of life.

When analyzing cultural membership and inclusion, we must have a full appre-ciation for what it means to belong. The best way to consider this is to think about your own sense of inclusion in the cultures in which you hold membership. Most everyone feels included in his or her cultures. The reason I know this is that most of us (unless you are a glutton for punishment) do not stay in cultures or communities where we do not feel welcomed.

How many times have you been pulled to a party by a friend who was invited, only to realize when you get there that you do not know a soul? As you grope and bumble around the party, you are really thinking about the easiest way to leave. We don't like to stay in places where we do not feel we belong.

This happened to me recently when I was invited to a gathering by a friend. This fellow is always game to participate when I invite him to my gatherings, so I could not say no to his invitation. I wasn't excited, but I thought it would not be that bad. When we arrived at the gathering, my friend knew most of those in attendance and began to circulate amongst his friends. I followed him around, sheepishly, hanging on to elements of his conversation. I couldn't wait to leave. Now understand, I am no retiring butterfly, but this setting was still awkward and I was uneasy and uncomfortable. I was "in" the party, but not "of" the party.

As we think about belonging and inclusion, let us reflect on those things that are tied to the concept. What is it that signals inclusion? How do you know when you belong to a group or culture? What happens in those experiences when you really feel included? When I pose this question in training sessions, I hear a variety of thoughts. People tell me that inclusion is tantamount to being welcomed, respected, honored, loved and involved.

For me, inclusion, belonging and community membership boil down to three major themes. These are:

- *Being Acknowledged*–This is when people reach out to you and see you as having something relevant to offer.
- *Being Appreciated*–We are appreciated when we feel valued to the point that others care about what we bring to the community.
- *Being Accepted*–To be accepted is to become a part of the community in a formal way–to be a player.

Perhaps the most illuminating example of inclusion for me came about in a most unexpected way. I found myself with a flight delay at the St. Louis Lambert Field. With plenty of time on my hands, and my reading material already devoured, I began roaming the airport to kill time. I happened upon the *Cheers* bar and decided to have something to eat. After my order was taken and I did a complete scan of the bar, I noticed that they were showing old reruns of the *Cheers* TV show on the monitors.

I have always been a fan of *Cheers*. Even now when I find an old episode on TV, I cannot resist watching. In fact, in a way, the storyline for *Cheers* fits well into the discussion of culture, community and inclusion. The storyline of *Cheers* revolves around six very eccentric characters who resonate well in spite of their odd behaviors. Indeed, their strange behavior is what makes the stories interesting. All six characters are acknowledged, appreciated and accepted regardless of how unusual they might be. This is true inclusion.

As I watched these episodes, it hit me like a ton of bricks. All of these characters belonged. They were included just as they are. The culture worked. Do you remember the *Cheers* theme song? If you do, you will recall that one of the lines is: "*I want to be where everyone knows my name; and they're always glad I came.*" This is the definition of belonging and inclusion–to be where people know our name and are glad we came. Cultural membership is a two-way street where we feel acknowledged, appreciated and accepted. It is a dynamic experience that affects our feelings. You always know in your gut if you are included.

In community membership, you can quickly observe degrees of involvement. There are those very active members, the ones who are always there and always in the front row. These people are deeply passionate about the cause and are always willing to help out. Next are semi-active members who come around, but are not as regular or quick to help. These folks observe more and will step to the plate if nudged or prompted, but their natural propensity is to be in the second row. The final group is that one found at the borders. These folks belong, but just barely. They often do not show up and usually never volunteer to do things. They might offer some advice from time to time, but are firmly planted in the last row.

Think of the communities of which you are a member and analyze your own level of participation. You are probably in one of these three rows in your communities. Now sometimes there are reasons you stay in the second or third row. It might be that your time is limited, or you are spread too thin. Another reason might be that you may not feel you know as much about the common theme that others might know. Or it might be that your general interest in the theme is just not that keen.

Along with how you position yourself in the community, the most critical aspect of membership is the social capital gained through the relationships you form with other members. These relationships create opportunities for the launching of connections that can satisfy all levels of need. That is, all of us look for and need a variety of relationships in our lives to keep us stable. From acquaintanceships that build important social bridging to close relationships that create deep personal bonding, the members of various communities that we belong to help fill these voids.

Whatever the issue, members of communities position themselves in various places within their groups in an effort to not only develop important relationships, but to also do the work that the community requests. This work plays out in the following elements.

Rituals

Any time two or more people come together with any regularity around a theme of mutual interest, one of the first things that occurs is the establishment of community rituals. A ritual is a deep-rooted behavior that the community holds as important. They are behaviors that have become so established in the culture that people hardly recognize them when they occur. But they do recognize when the behaviors drift away or when people begin to ignore the rituals.

Every culture has a myriad of rituals that are unique to how the members celebrate their common theme. One easy way to think about rituals is to consider the typical family. All of our families have rituals that define who we are. These rituals happen all the time, but the most evident revolve around holidays and family ceremonies. Religious holiday rituals present clear examples. In my family, Christmas Eve is full of deep rituals, from the formal dinner complete with various fishes and Italian delicacies, to the gift exchange with my parents, now in their eighties. Then off to Christmas Eve services at Mother of Sorrows Church where we celebrate the Mass, complete with the Italian carol, *El Tunde de La Stella*. After Mass, we begin house-to-house visits late into the evening.

Rituals can be formal or informal, but they are always important to the culture. Think about the rituals that play out at your work site. Each of us follows predictable routines that define our culture. Add these individual rituals into the broader activities of the worksite, and there is the creation of a clear culture.

One important element about rituals is that they are serious issues. Even if they seem silly or funny from afar, they represent serious business to the members of the culture. Members of the culture often put people who mock or disregard their rituals in uncomfortable positions. I remember an experience that happened a few years ago that illustrates this. I was in Minneapolis with an evening free. Being a big baseball fan, I decided to head into town to see the Twins play at the Metrodome. I arrived at the stadium and made my way to the cheap seats and waited for the game to begin.

Baseball is a culture with deep and historic roots. You can predict many things and look forward to them being a part of the game. There was a small crowd, maybe 10,000 or so fans on hand, and right before the game was to begin, a classic baseball ritual occurred. The announcer came on the PA system and said: "*Ladies and gentlemen, will you please rise for the national anthem. Gentleman, take off your hats to honor America.*" At that point, all the fans rose to participate in a baseball ritual. I noticed that sitting a few rows behind me were two teenage boys, dressed in the "grunge" look–baggy pants, oversize sweatshirts and ball caps, turned sideways. These fellows were still in their seats with feet propped on the row in front of them. They were talking and clearly ignoring the ritual until two rather large "cultural enforcers" walked over to them and suggested they stand up. The boys hesitated until an "enforcer" lifted one of them up. Both boys quickly took off their caps and the four of them sang the national anthem together.

Most of us remember the original *Planet of the Apes* movies from the late '60s and early '70s. These movies presented a stark portrayal of rituals when humans observed the formal behaviors of the apes. Some of them seemed bizarre, but the director was actually illustrating human cultural rituals. As the heroes of the movie watched the apes do religious or patriotic rituals, it reflected on how strange some of our rituals might seem to alien cultures.

Rituals are important because they soon become norms in a community. As behaviors harden, the culture becomes more influenced by them. Interestingly, the rituals or norms of a group or culture can be positive, negative or neutral in how they impact the culture's future. For instance, some behaviors that become rituals that have a negative effect can lead to the demise of the culture. An example is in the culture of some gangs. As the gangs develop rituals for their members that are destructive, these behaviors can lead to arrests and a breakup of the gang. Conversely, if a culture develops behaviors that are positive for the group, these rituals will work to strengthen and bond the community.

Beyond the impact on cultures or communities, individuals also develop rituals and norms that are hardened into routines. Think about your own routines. A good one to reflect on might be your morning routine. If you are like most people, you probably have a very structured pattern in which you follow deeply set rituals. Your morning coffee and paper, feeding the dog or birds and walking around your house before you head off to work are all examples of rituals. It really doesn't matter how formal or informal they are, these rituals soon become important to you.

Rituals for groups or communities often can be categorized or clustered. For example, countries have patriotic rituals that many communities honor. One example relevant to me right now is Memorial Day. Soon I will attend a Memorial Day parade that my son's little league team will be marching in. This ritual is done yearly to try to pass on the importance of patriotic sacrifice to our children. Even though the kids seem more interested in the treats given after the parade, the community hopes that some of the symbolism of the event will rub off on them.

Religious rituals are equally interesting to observe. Various religious groups perform rituals that signal a direct or symbolic message about their religion. In the Roman Catholic religion that I practice, one interesting ritual is the sign of the cross. When I was a small boy, I remember my dad teaching me to make the sign of the cross as I entered church and at various times during the Mass. I didn't really know what it meant, but I did know that it was important. And the more I did it like everyone else, the easier it was to be a part of the community.

Communities and cultures also develop social rituals that become important. Years ago I was involved in creating a volleyball league for human services professionals in Pittsburgh. The HSVL (Human Service Volleyball League) as it was called, became a very defined community. It began in 1974 with ten teams, and has now grown to thirty teams in three divisions. The culture has ebbed and flowed over these past years, but one ritual that is still honored is the Wednesday night social gathering. Since 1974, Wednesday nights have been the evening for socializing and getting to know the members better. This ritual started because we played only on Wednesdays and after the games we would all go out for drinks. Today the league plays on various nights, but Wednesday is still the social night.

Just the other day I was called to reflect on the rituals that bonded a community of which I was a member while in college. When I arrived home from work I found a newsletter from my fraternity, Alpha Phi Delta. It made me recall when I found myself in a social dilemma as a college freshman in the mid-1960s. My two high school chums that I went off to college with left after our first freshman semester; I lost my two apartment roommates and my only established friendship network. As I struggled to reconnect, I was drawn to Alpha Phi Delta fraternity. At the time, Alpha Phi Delta was a national Italian fraternity with an all-Italian membership. Coming from an Italian family with deep ethnic roots, I was drawn to APD. Soon I became a member, but not without a long, ritualistic pledge period. During this time we were taught the rituals and information that bonded the brotherhood. It has been a long time since I have reflected on my fraternity years, but as I turned the pages of the Alpha Phi Delta newsletter I was called back, as if it was yesterday, to the rituals that bonded us in brotherhood. We had all the key elements of a culture, but it is the rituals that I most easily remember.

Much more could be said about rituals, but suffice it to say that rituals are important to understanding cultures and communities. If you are interested in joining or influencing a culture, knowing and honoring the rituals is an important first step. The only way new people become valued in a culture is when they come to know and then practice the rituals.

Patterns

The patterns of a culture refer to the movements and territory of the members of the community. Make no mistake about it–human beings and the cultures we create are not only ritualistic, but highly territorial as well. In fact, in many ways we are not that far removed from our animal neighbors who mark their territory with scent or action. Have you ever reflected on how you feel when someone sits at your desk, uninvited, and begins to use your phone or sort through your stuff? This sense of territoriality can cause us to become angry or anxious.

In a larger context, the notion of territory has been the cause for rifts, skirmishes and wars. Nations have come to blows over territorial invasions or reaching over boundaries. I remember my first trip to Europe years ago and the stark contrast from one border to another. On this trip, when our tour bus came to a border, it was not uncommon for heavily armed guards to enter the bus and demand we show our passports. Territory is important to people and communities. And today, this era of terrorism has led to the concept of "homeland security." We work hard to safeguard our borders from those who might want to destroy our way of life. All over the world, people struggle to find safety in their home or community and have begun to fear anything that suggests a difference from that which they know.

One can inspect the patterns of movement of cultural members (patterning) and learn vital information on the importance and prominence of the members. This type of observation becomes important when we try to identify gatekeepers and other critical cultural connectors. Another important manifestation of patterning is how people continue to revolve around the territory they have come to know. A powerful example here is to think about your church, synagogue or temple. If you worship on a regular basis, you probably have your own pew. I know for the Condeluci family this is true. We have come into the habit of attending 9:00 Mass every Sunday, and unless there is some serious change in world affairs, you can place a bet on where we are going to sit. All the other parishioners understand this because they have their own pews as well.

Think about your own social movements with communities in which you hold membership. If the community has regular meetings, you probably position yourself in the same space at most meetings. This is commonplace for most of us. Things become awkward when you penetrate into a new community for the first time. In these experiences you have to sort out where to locate yourself, and this is no easy task. Most of us stumble and bumble until we see someone we know or feel some connection.

The notion of patterning also takes cultural space into account. Cultural space refers to the direct distance between cultural members. Anthropologists have suggested there are three major space dimensions that play out with groups. These are:

1. *Public Space*–the formal distance between people when a cultural meeting is taking place. The people running the meeting or the invited speaker position themselves somewhat apart from the members. Public space is usually five or more feet.

2. *Social Space*–the typical distances between cultural members when they are socializing or talking amongst themselves. This space is from two to five feet.

3. *Intimate Space*–the close and personal space that is reserved for covenant or licensed relationships, or those relationships that deal with great joy or sorrow. This is the space between lovers, or with people who have a license to be close, like doctors or barbers. Or, during times of great joy or sorrow, community members might hug or hold onto each other. Intimate space ranges from touching to a one-foot distance.

Patterning also refers to the location that the culture meets or celebrates in. This location drives how the culture relates and the decisions that members make in relationship to space. For example, when your spiritual community meets at church, synagogue or temple, you take your regular pew. But, if the congregation has a picnic or gathering in a different venue, this new location will have an impact on the patterning. This change can create a sense of disharmony until the congregation settles in with the new location. What typically happens is that members who sit near each other in church will gravitate toward each other at the new location.

Jargon

Jargon refers to the words, phrases or lexicon the culture uses to discuss, debate or celebrate the common theme. All cultures, informal or formal, establish words that have meaning only to them. These words can be slang, acronyms or "pet words." The key is that they are meaningful to members of the culture.

Informal cultures like families use a battery of words to describe people, events or things. Often these words (or phrases) have clear meaning to us, but seem silly or strange to others who may overhear us talk. Sometimes these words are ethnic, symbolic or reflective of some past experience or event. My family, for example, uses a number of Italian sayings or words that would seem alien to any outsider. In fact, not very long ago a friend from Toronto was visiting our agency and I invited him to a family gathering. As we sat down for dinner I realized he did not have a napkin at his place setting and called out to my wife to bring in a "mopine." From the look on my friend's face, he was sure that Liz would be bringing in a mop for him. The word "mopine" is an Italian word that means napkin or face cloth. We use it all the time in our family, but my Canadian friend had never heard it before.

Communication theory looks at the notion of coding and decoding of messages as the heart of the communication process. Coding refers to how messages are constructed. When we code a message, we are attempting to utilize words and delivery in a way that will enhance the possibility that the person receiving the message will understand it. A good communicator will try to better understand the sphere of experience of the person with whom he or she is communicating. The more you know about the person's world, the easier coding will be. To this extent, jargon can come into play in communication theory. When I meet new people, if I find an area they are keen on, I might code some of my message with jargon that corresponds. This will probably enhance my message.

Another type of informal jargon uses the "hip" or "in" words or phrases of the culture. This type of jargon may not facilitate the culture doing its work, but signals that the person is a member. Popular words or phrases can come and go. Magazines and newspapers will often identify the "in" and "out" words or phrases of the popular culture. Often these lists are published at the end of a year, helping members of the culture know what jargon to use in the New Year.

I often rely on my children to help me learn the new hip words of the culture. Usually, however, when I begin to apply the words, my kids will laugh and make fun of me. Word utilization is an interesting issue of jargon. Many times a newcomer to the culture might use the wrong word, or apply the word inappropriately. When this happens, the newcomer can be held at bay by the culture as an imposter. This can lead to exclusion. My failed use of the hip words provided by my children signals me as an imposter to that culture.

More formal cultures use words that are technical or focused on their work or business. These words or phrases can be descriptive or explanatory, and the sooner people in the culture know them the easier it is for them to do the work of the culture. In many companies, new staff members are given a glossary of words to help them navigate in communications.

Good examples of this are the new words ushered in by the high technology information society. First used by players in the world of computers and software, words like gigabyte, hard drive, ram, Internet, server and modem are being more popularly applied as computers become more accessible. These words, first a part of a formal culture, are now found in other domains as well. Such jargon begins to transcend its parochial culture to be applied across the board.

Regardless of the formal or informal notions of the culture, the jargon is critical for members of the culture to do their work. To understand and then apply the jargon is a key ingredient to cultural belonging.

Memory

Another dimension of any culture or community is the notion of memory. Simply applied, memory refers to the history and legacy of the community or culture. Memory captures and retains key elements of the past that get passed on to current members to help them maintain and retain the elements of the culture. To this extent, memory can revolve around any of the cultural aspects reviewed in this section. Memory can include stories, photos or folklore of the common theme, rituals, patterns or jargon of the culture.

The capturing of a culture's memory can be addressed formally or informally. For example, formal cultures keep track of their past through things like yearbooks, annual reports, newsletters, bulletins and the like. These official publications do honor to the past and help keep current members committed. Through stories and photos these agents of memory serve as glue for the culture.

Recently, my daughter Gianna received her high school yearbook. Gianna is a member of the yearbook staff and as a sophomore has responsibility to help plan and organize next year's edition. We sat together to look at the publication, and she explained to me all the rituals that were captured in the pages. The yearbook was indexed with the name of each student and the pages in the book where photos of that person could be found. Gianna showed me the most popular students and how many pages were listed after their names. She was sensitive to the fact that she would like to have more pages listed by her name, and she told me that she was going to sign up for more activities in the coming year. The function of the index seemed to be to list each student's impact on the school culture. For Gianna, this was an impetus for her (and other students, I am sure) to sign up to do more things at their school. Members of cultures, be they schools, or families or churches, want to be remembered. This drive for memory pushes people to commit more deeply to the culture.

In fact, some of the most powerful aspects of memory are found with photos, stories or folklore, regardless of whether they are formal or informal. Think about your family to better understand the potency of photos and stories to memory. For my family, the photos that have captured any of our history are deeply revered. We have created scrapbooks of all the children's births, and each critical stepping stone. Add to this the vacations and other family events, and you have a flood of photos that create a deep and intense memory for all of us in the family. During a recent visit to one of my cousins, I discovered that she was taking a scrapbook class. The class taught her how to not only keep photos of her family, but to enhance their display by adding images and colors to enhance and focus the impact of the photos. These scrapbooks offered an exciting point of memory for her family for their future.

Stories too are key elements of memory in a culture. Every culture has its stories and folklore that relate to its past. These types of memories continue to underscore the viability of the culture. For example, at my agency, stories from the past flow every time we have a gathering. People reflect on things they did, others who came before them and other people who had an impact on the culture.

These stories are critical because they not only pay homage to the past, but also give the current members something to strive for within the culture. As current members relive past events, they set the bar for behaviors that might elevate themselves to the status of being a part of a future story. Just as with Gianna's yearbook, if the culture remembers you, your importance in the culture is established. In a way, stories cement the past and set a promise for the future.

Perhaps the strongest role that memory plays in a culture is the evolution of wisdom. As the members of the community remember things, this memory leads to a sense of understanding. The wisdom of a community greatly solidifies the potential for community survival and success.

Gatekeepers

In any discussion of culture or community, especially one that examines change, the most critical ingredient is the gatekeeper. The gatekeeper is defined as an indigenous member of the culture, or someone already included and accepted in the culture, who has some formal or informal influence within the culture. That is, the person has either official (elected or selected) leadership, or is unofficially endorsed by colleagues and influential in the culture. Either way, the gatekeeper has authority and influence with the members.

Gatekeepers can be positive or negative in how they see new people, products or ideas. The positive gatekeeper is accepting, open and willing to take risks. Conversely, the negative gatekeeper is closed and rejects new things. Thus, the positive gatekeeper opens the culture to new things and the negative gatekeeper attempts to protect the existing culture and maintain the status quo. When there are multiple gatekeepers, they typically fall into a classic bell-shaped curve in which about 20% have the propensity to be positive, with another 20% being negative. The remaining 60% tend to be neutral and could be swayed either way, depending on the influence and energy of dominant gatekeepers.

Although some people tend to be hard-core positive or negative, sometimes people can be positive or negative on an issue-by-issue basis. A person who tends to be positive might be a negative gatekeeper on an issue he or she feels strongly about. This tendency to adjust according to the issue adds a complexity to the notion of gatekeeping. We all probably know some people who are usually receptive to new ideas, products or people, but on certain issues seem to be fully closed.

Often gatekeepers are the formally sanctioned leaders of the culture. These are people who have official power within the community. This could be the mayor of a city, the governor of a state, the supervisor of the team or the president of the club. Because these people have recognized power, they can be formidable gatekeepers. Beyond this, however, are those people in every community who do not have formal power but are very influential with the other members. These unofficial leaders are gatekeepers as well. A good example here is the storyline of the book *M*A*S*H*, by Richard Hooker. In this book (and in the subsequent movie and TV series), the character of Radar O'Reilly served as a gatekeeper. Radar was the one who could get things done. He could get olives for the martinis when supplies had been cut off. He could get the score of the World Series when there was radio blackout. He could secure a weekend pass when the surgeons needed that break. In fact, he ran the *M*A*S*H* unit. Radar was a key gatekeeper in this community even though he did not hold an officer's rank.

The reason gatekeepers are critical to culture is that they can use their power to endorse or reject a new idea, person or product to the culture. This action, in turn, can influence the 60% of cultural members who have not decided or thought about the new issue. A good example of how this works is to think about political endorsements. When a candidate develops publicity for a campaign, he or she often solicits a celebrity to endorse the candidacy, or to speak against the opponent. In this process, gatekeepers attempt to promote their candidate and help to reject the opponent. The hope is that the gatekeeper will influence the undecided voters to support a candidate.

Advertisers on Madison Avenue understand the potency of the gatekeeper. Whenever companies decide to introduce a new product to the culture, they use the power of advertising to promote their product. The most critical phase is the initial penetration of the product into the culture. Although advertising firms are creative in this process, one of the most time-tested methods is to have the product introduced by a celebrity or influential person. As the celebrity pitches the product, the members of the community who are exposed to the advertising often are drawn first to the celebrity, and then to the product. Indeed, some products become so associated with celebrities that they put their names on the product. Basketball shoes are a perfect example. It seems that every major professional player has his or her own shoes on the market. Of course, the markup on these endorsed products is great. I know this all too well, because I have two sons who wanted to "be like Mike" by having Michael Jordan sneakers.

A key to the success of this approach to influence the culture is that the gatekeeper must continue to keep his or her positive appeal in the culture. One example of the twists and turns that can happen is O. J. Simpson. Not long ago, Simpson was the darling of the advertising world. He had everything companies wanted–he was handsome, well off, an excellent athlete who had made the transition to actor and a family man as well. Simpson was everywhere: on TV, billboards, magazines and other media outlets. Then came the murders for which he was arrested in California. Even though a jury acquitted Simpson of the murders, he is a *persona non grata* in the advertising world today. His gatekeeper image was indelibly tarnished.

We can see examples of gatekeepers in all walks of life. One example is the religious ceremony of baptism. In a baptism, a newcomer to the religion is formally welcomed into the congregation. Through a symbolic ceremony, the person is anointed and then formally announced to the congregation. Standing by the person being baptized is the sponsor, or godparent. The other members of the congregation usually know this gatekeeper. When they stand with and for the newcomer, they essentially transfer their status to the newcomer. In the Disney movie, *The Lion King*, when the lion cub Simba is born, it is the highly valued Rafeiki who lifts Simba up to all of the animal kingdom to announce his arrival. This, too, is a type of baptism.

This transition of values is a powerful signal. The congregation knows and values the godparents and minister. As these valued gatekeepers stand with the newcomer, the value of the newcomer goes up in the eyes of the congregation. Not that the newcomer is fully embraced, but at least he or she gets a ledgehold in the new culture. The gatekeeper gives enough starting value to the new person that he or she can begin the process of cultural penetration.

Think about the many gatekeepers you have had in your life as you have made your way into community. Consider the clubs you have joined, the times you moved to a new place, taken a new job or went to a gathering of your life partner's families for the first time. No matter where or when, a gatekeeper played a role in helping you get into the group. If this didn't happen, you probably left or bailed out. Quite simply, we rarely get into cultures without the assistance of a gatekeeper.

One simple gatekeeper activity that happens often with me occurs when I am invited to speak. No matter the venue, my presentation is initiated by a personal introduction. A valued member of the culture who is known to those in attendance introduces me. This person serves as my gatekeeper. In essence he or she sanctions my being there and urges those in attendance to listen to what I will be saying. This process creates an initial value rise for the message and for me, and sets the tone for the penetration of my message to the audience.

The Positive Gatekeeper

Gatekeepers, especially positive gatekeepers, are critical to culture, because they help bring new things into the community. When they do this, the new idea, person or product introduced by the gatekeeper causes the existing members of the culture to define or redefine their position on the matter. This addition and redefinition of culture is what leads to cultural growth.

This is how cultural shifting occurs. When the positive gatekeeper introduces a new item, the other members of the culture begin to weigh in on the item. Negative gatekeepers will try to challenge the new thing. This may happen overtly or covertly. As positive and negative gatekeepers make their points, the other 60% of the culture pays attention. As others begin to sign on, the culture either begins to shift toward the new thing or reject it outright and go back to where it was. This is the essence of cultural shifting.

This very phenomenon played out with my family recently. While out for a weekend shopping expedition, I asked my family where they would like to go for lunch. My youngest boy, Santino, was quick to tell us about a new restaurant that he saw advertised on TV. He thought we might like to try it.

Immediately my older son, Dante, said, "*No, no, no, why don't we just go to EatnPark. We always go there and we know the menu. Everyone will find something they like.*"

Santino objected and said, "*We always go to EatnPark. Let's try something new for a change.*"

As Dante and Santino traded opinions, my daughter, my wife and I listened to the banter. In essence we (60% of the family) would consider the merits of the arguments and make the ultimate decision, because we consisted of the critical mass to shift the culture. (We ended up at the new place, by the way.)

Anthropologists also have studied this phenomenon. Homogeneity, or similarity of members of culture, creates a sense of comfort and security for the group. Everyone has the same things to resonate around and embrace. Heterogeneity, or the convergence of differences, pushes the culture to growth. Difference causes us to grow.

In his book, *The Tipping Point* (2000), Malcolm Gladwell reflects on the kinds of people and events necessary to move something from fad to mainstream. He called this key element of transfer a tipping point. In his work he describes the types of people who move ideas, people or products into the mainstream. He calls these folks connectors, mavens and salesmen.

- The "connectors" are the people with broad circles, who can influence a lot of these people. They are unique because their circles extend beyond the usual parochial boundaries.
- The "mavens" are people who have information and are always looking to share this information with others. Mavens get nothing for their information. They share important and useful things because they enjoy helping people.
- The "salesmen" are passionate purveyors of ideas, products or people. Salesmen may not necessarily have deep relationships, but they have the opportunity to share things.

Gatekeepers are people with one, two or all three of these qualities. They are the key to cultural shifting because they promote or reject things that push the community to a new level. The way that they influence the culture can be either positive, where they support and endorse a new person, idea or product; or negative, where they oppose it.

Over the years anthropologists have attempted to examine what type of people lead to social change and cultural shifting. As new things help to develop or enhance the existing culture, the elements of positive gatekeepers become important to understand. Some of the things we do know about positive gatekeepers are:

- They tend to be positive people. They genuinely like people and look for the good in everyone they meet.
- They are social risk-takers. They reach out to the underdog and are willing to take cultural flack if need be.
- They reach out to new things and are curious and interested in why, how and why not.
- They tend to be younger people and not so caught up in dogma.
- More often than not they tend to be women. Men are usually more conservative and become more easily set in their ways.
- They are highly social and tend to be good mixers.
- They tend to have respected influence with their community.

Positive gatekeepers are absolutely essential for diffusion of new ideas, products or people to penetrate into an existing community. To this extent the positive gatekeeper is akin to the innovators and early adopters mentioned earlier.

The Negative Gatekeeper

Any analysis of gatekeepers would be remiss if negative gatekeepers were not explored. We know that those who resist or fight change are active members of the culture. These are often the people who usually are negative in their thinking. The ultimate negative gatekeepers can include the people who reject or hate other people, and the bigots and racists of our society.

Although it is difficult to nail down percentages, some psychologists suggest that close to 20% of any community consists of people who are highly negative in general. In fact, some analysts think that this number might be higher. They attribute this to the fact that most children are raised in our society today in a way that promotes a negative perspective. It has been estimated that before a child reaches his eighteenth year, he or she hears the word "no" 148,000 times. Couple this with the win-or-lose mentality promoted by competition in sports and scholastics, it is no wonder that most children develop a negative outlook on life. This sadly translates to our popular culture. Some estimates hold that 75% of the stories published in newspapers or appear on TV have a negative flair. Could it be that 75% of everything we think is negative?

This perseveration on negativity has an effect on how members of communities relate to new ideas, products and people. These types of cautions and fears can create formidable resistance to change. It is easier for people to be or drift toward negative gatekeepers than to be positive or innovative as it relates to change. To this extent, the task of the positive gatekeeper is very challenging.

Assertive or Unassertive Gatekeepers

Along with the positive and negative framework for gatekeepers, one also can be assertive or unassertive. The assertive gatekeeper is one who initiates their positive or negative perspective on the new person, product or idea without any requests or prompts. These are people who give their opinion without anyone asking for it. They are quick to endorse or reject the new thing. All of us know people who meet this description. They are similar to Gladwell's perspective on "mavens." These are the people who automatically have an opinion on things, sometimes regardless of how much they really know about them.

On the opposite side are those who are more cautious on expressing their opinion, be it positive or negative. Because they are deliberate, they may be mistaken for the 60% of community who tend to follow. Yet these folks are not followers. They have developed opinions, but they do not readily share them unless they are asked or feel compelled. In a way, the unassertive gatekeepers are "wild cards" in the process of cultural shifting because they hold back. Often it is not until these individuals make their opinions known that the more neutral people begin to take a stand. This can create the official shift for endorsement or rejection.

▲

The notion of the gatekeeper is clearly a critical piece in thinking about cultural shifting. The only way culture changes or adapts is when the positive gatekeeper, whether assertive or unassertive, brings new things into the fray. They are the innovators and early adopters of new ideas, products or people being introduced to community. To this extent, if change is to happen, positive gatekeepers will be at the core.

Community and Relationships

The key to understanding communities is to appreciate how relationships develop and grow. Since all communities are dependent on relationships, the more we know about the human condition of relationship-building, the closer we can get to helping the culture shift in ways that we desire.

We know that relationships flow from acquaintanceships to the deepest form of relationships. This flow can be clear when we think about our own lives and the various people we have relationships with. One interesting exercise is to develop a sociogram of your life. Such a map would start with identifying all the critical relationships in your life. For most of us, these deep relationships will include family and close loved ones and probably will total ten to fifteen people. In fact, most of us will not typically have more than fifteen intimate people, because these types of close relationships take a lot of time and energy. Psychologists call this level of relationships our "sympathy group."

After our sympathy group comes our friendship network. These are the people we have come to know through our interests and participation in activities. These people can be close to us, or more distant as acquaintances. But either way, they are friends and we share something in common.

The final circle to any sociogram would be the acquaintances you have in your life. Here we would list the various people we know. Many of these people would include those you pay to have in your life. This might be the barber or beautician you employ, or the bank teller you know, or your doctor. You have a relationship with these people, but typically you pay to have them be in your life.

All told, when anthropologists ask people to identify the whole gamut of relationships in their lives, the average number that gets reported is about one hundred-fifty people. This number meshes with one theory of relationships developed by anthropologist Robin Dunbar. Dunbar developed an equation for relationships among members of a species, called the neocortex ratio, or the size of the neocortex relative to the size of the brain. For humans this figure is approximately one hundred forty-eight, which represents the maximum number of people with whom humans can have meaningful relationships. Due to brain size and complexity, this is the largest group of relationships among primates.

Consequently human relationships define the essence of community. Most people have relationships that can grow to an average of about one hundred-fifty, of which fifteen or so will be intimate relationships. These types of data are interesting and useful in thinking about cultural shifting. The more we know about community and relationships the closer we can get to influencing the new things that can cause the culture to grow.

The Decline of Community

Any study of the notion of culture and community would be remiss if it did not look at current trends on the strength of community. As much as we would like to believe that community continues to grow and develop in positive ways, the truth is that statistics suggest otherwise. As sociologists attempt to get a picture of community they are discovering some trends that point to community decline.

Over the last twenty-five years the percentage of people surveyed who say they regularly have dinner with their own families has decreased by a full third. Similarly, vacationing with the full family is down a third, as well as the time we spend together in front of the TV, which is also down a third, even as TV watching is increasing.

In his book, *Bowling Alone* (2000), sociologist Robert Putnam chronicled this downward spiral. Some of the data he reports are:

From 1974 to 1994 the following civic actions have dropped:

- 42% less people served as a club officer
- 42% less people worked for a political party
- 39% less people served on a civic committee
- 35% less people attended a public meeting
- 34% less people attended a political rally or speech
- overall, 32 million fewer Americans participate in formal communities

In addition, he found church attendance down from 46% in 1960 to 36% in 1999; trade association membership declined from 70% in 1960 to 40% in 1999; playing cards with friends dropped from sixteen times per year in 1975 to eight times in 1999; bowlers who bowled in leagues dropped from 82% of bowlers in 1960 to only 21% in 1999.

Sociologists who follow the ebb and flow of community have concluded that most indicators of community have been on the decline since 1960. This decline has been vivid in the patterns of formal and informal joining. From activities such as going on picnics to officially joining a formal political party, all are on a steep decline. This trend has caused social scientists to reflect on the reasons why. After a vigorous review, Putnam and his associates conclude the following four themes that have led to the serious decline of community. These are, in order of importance:

- the slow, steady replacement of a civic generation by their less involved children and grandchildren
- electronic entertainment, especially television
- pressures of time and money, including the special pressures on two-career families
- suburbanization, commuting and sprawl

Given these aspects of culture and community, from the notions that define community to an understanding of our current cultural trends, we are now ready to think about cultural shifting. By using the elements of community and the realities of community today, we can begin to harness the way community comes to do its business. As positive gatekeepers introduce new people, ideas or products into the community, a ledgehold is established for cultural shifting.

This chapter has taken a broad look at culture and community. If we can identify the common themes and interests that people with disabilities have and then look at the ingredients of community, this process will offer a much more optimistic opportunity for community inclusion. The balance of this book does just this.

HUMANS ARE THE ONLY SPECIES WHO IS NOT LOCKED INTO THEIR ENVIRONMENT. THEIR IMAGINATION, REASON, EMOTIONAL SUBTLETY AND TOUGHNESS, MAKE IT POSSIBLE FOR THEM TO NOT ONLY ACCEPT THE ENVIRONMENT, BUT TO CHANGE IT. — JACOB BRONOWSKI

CHAPTER 3
Principles of Cultural Shifting

To study culture and community is one thing, but to put the principles of cultural shifting into place is quite another. In this section we will look at how the elements of culture can be utilized by change agents to promote a shifting and adjustment. We will examine this approach primarily out of a framework of shifting a culture to assist disconnected people to enter a community.

The Bridge to Joining a Culture

The challenge of cultural shifting is more clearly understood when thinking of the concept of a bridge. Bridges are interesting structures. They blend two important notions: the simplicity of connecting two points and the complexity of the engineering necessary to make the connection. This blending is apparent in the example of a change agent attempting to foster the inclusion of people with disabilities in the mainstream of the community. The challenge is simple, but the complexity in making it happen is difficult.

To understand this example, however, we must appreciate the powerful forces of exclusion that precede the challenge. Historically, people with disabilities have been perceived out of a medical model of deficiency and dysfunction. In *Interdependence: The Route to Community* (1991) and *Beyond Difference* (1996), I explored the effects of the medical model and the stigma of difference that have created formidable cultural realities leading to community devaluation. In these books I made the point that the medical treatment model has resulted in people with disabilities being seen in the context of inability, problems or incapability.

Using the metaphor of a river, the change agent can think of the individual with a disability as being on one side of a river and the community on the other. The goal for rehabilitation is to assist the person with the disability to move over the river, from being excluded to joining the community at large. Thus, the river is the gap between the person and the community, representing the problems or deficiencies the person is seen as having. Figure 1 shows the current reality of the medical model of deficiency and dysfunction.

Figure I
The Medical Approach to Disability

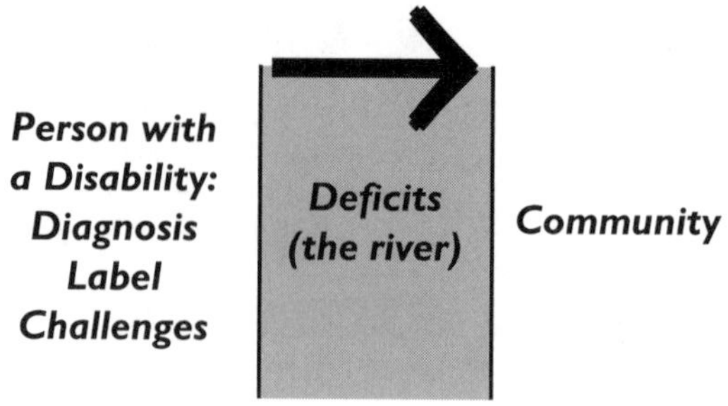

*Person with
a Disability:
Diagnosis
Label
Challenges*
 | *Deficits
(the river)* | Community

The medical model suggests that the best way to get people from one side of the illustration to the other is to focus on the problem: the disability. In most human services programs this is exactly how the issue of inclusion is addressed. Conventional wisdom says that we try to mitigate the differences so that the person can be more easily included into the community. This conventional view is a linear approach to the inclusion of people with disabilities. It suggests that if we can fix the problem, we can more easily get the person included. The major target for change is the person with the difference.

Although this approach has been practiced for years, in essence it has not led to real community inclusion for the vast majority of people with disabilities. We have moved people into the community but not really helped them become of the community. To continue to position the person with the disability as the problem and to try to change him or her is to chase the wrong butterfly. What is needed is a shifting of culture.

Rather than putting an emphasis on the person and focusing attention on his or her differences, I am suggesting that we rethink the approach. Consider the example of a disconnection between two points. Much like our illustration above, if you find yourself at point A and you are interested in getting to point B, but there is a river in your way, you might see the river as a problem. To this end, one could seek out help from an engineer as to how we might get rid of the river so that we can pass to point B safely. In some ways this is how the medical model frames the problem of inclusion for people with disabilities. It suggests that the way to get people included in the community is to fix the problems they have. That is, fill in the river!

However, if we re-frame the problem to simply crossing the river, the challenge changes from seeing the river as a problem to thinking what other ways we might safely pass over. The focus turns to what it might take to build a bridge. In this shift of thinking, the river is not a problem, but a reality to be addressed based on the strength and stability of the shorelines where we plan to anchor the bridge. Consequently, the more important factors are not the problem posed by the river, but the strength that can be garnered to build the bridge. (See Figure 2.)

Figure 2
Community Approach to Disability

Person with a Disability:
Passions
Dreams
Skills
Capacities
Potential

Community

Commonalities and Connections (the bridge)

To this end, to create a real shift in culture follows this metaphor of a bridge. This demands that the change agent think about four critical steps. These steps are contrary to the medical model and, in many ways, contrary to how the human services system relates to people with disabilities. However, for the most part, this is probably the way we can get people truly included in the community.

Four Steps to Cultural Shifting

When considering how any new person, product or idea can be incorporated into the existing culture, the following four steps are always present. As we explore these steps, keep in mind how they may have worked for you as you have attempted to incorporate anything new into your community.

Step 1: Find the passion or point of connection.
Step 2: Find the venue or play point.
Step 3: Understand the elements of culture.
Step 4: Enlist the gatekeeper.

Step 1: Find the Passion or Point of Connection

As with our bridge metaphor, finding the key points of strength and passion is the first step to cultural shifting. To build a strong bridge we must have a solid foundation to assure the bridge will be safe for passage. The passage of people, products or ideas into culture all require strength. To this end we must identify all that is strong or positive about that which we hope to shift the culture into embracing.

For people, this means we look for the following characteristics:

- passions
- interests
- dreams
- talents

- capacities
- hopes
- skills
- fantasies

- propensities
- avocations
- hobbies
- strengths

When we find these things in people, it helps us to support them. When a passion is identified in a person, the acknowledgment of this passion is empowering. Empowerment is a feeling we get when we are relevant and respected. People like to talk about that which they enjoy, and this also is uplifting.

Contrast this with a focus on people's problems or deficiencies. When you identify problems, especially those that are difficult to address or erase, this action is actually disempowering. You never feel good about the things you cannot do or do not do well.

This negative perspective, however, is exactly the way our human services system deals with difference or disability. When a person with a disability is referred to a human services agency, the first thing that happens is a formal assessment of the person's problems. These assessments are performed with detailed tests and reports. Once the problems are identified and labeled, an individualized program plan (IPP) is developed. Most often the effort is to fix the person's problem.

This deficiency model creates a negative slant and skews the process. It causes people to think negatively and critically about their reality. Further, serious frustration can occur if the problem really cannot be fixed. In many ways this is not the route to empowerment. In fact, focusing on our problems continues to bait negativity and set the tone for a poor self-image.

The capacity process suggests the exact opposite. By looking for those things that are positive and strength-oriented, we can help people build on those capacities they already have and promote their relevancy to the community. The same is true with products or ideas. When we look for and find the positive elements of ideas or products, we signal the initial points of connection of these things to the greater community and we are more apt to get others to embrace them. That is why advertisers stress the positive aspects of their products.

I had an experience a number of years ago that drove this contrast of positive and negative issues home. I was attending a symposium in Baltimore. It was the first day of a three-day gathering and people from all over the country were taking their seats in the meeting room. I scanned the room and didn't know a soul. As soon as the presenter came into the room he asked everyone to take out a sheet of paper. He asked us to write the word "positives" on the top of the page and to privately identify as many good things about ourselves as we could. Folks looked around at each other and then started in on the task. Within five minutes the presenter again got our attention and asked us to take out another sheet of paper. This time he told us to write the word "negatives" on the top and fill in as many problems, deficits or struggles we have. Again people got right into the task.

At this point the presenter asked for a volunteer to illustrate some points. I made eye contact with the presenter and he pointed to me. "*Sir, please stand up and pass your positive list to the person to your right,*" he said. I complied with the request and passed my "positive" list to the person to my right. To this person I did not know, the presenter said, "*Please introduce this man to your left, using his list as a guide.*" This person stood up and began to introduce me by referring to the good things I had written about myself. I smiled sheepishly and looked around at these unknown people as I was being introduced. Shaking his head affirmatively, the presenter then looked back at me and asked that I now pass my "negative" list to the person to my left. I paused, and then hesitantly handed my second list to the person to my left. Again, an introduction occurred by the stranger to my left, this time using my "negative" items. As this new introduction occurred, I can't begin to convey how vulnerable and naked I felt. I did not know these people, and as they came to know me through my problems and struggles, I felt embarrassed and ashamed.

In many cases, people know their passions and interests and are quick to tell you if you seem to be looking for the positives. With other folks you have to dig. In the work we do within the agency I direct, we often meet people with disabilities who have been so sheltered or inexperienced that they do not readily display their passions. Some people have been so devalued that they cannot seem to find their passions at all. In these types of situations, we must give the time and space necessary for people to identify those points of connections. This happens only when people feel valued and respected. It also happens when we welcome and include those who have a history with the person to help uncover the passions. Families or other relations have been invaluable for the capacity-building work we try to do in Pittsburgh.

This process is the same one we try to use with our children. One of our primary efforts as parents is to discover the interests and capacities of our children so as to connect them to communities that celebrate those same interests. Often this is a discovery process. This past spring my wife and I spent a Saturday cleaning out our garage. As we found and removed old bikes, cameras, hockey sticks, baseball bats, a ballerina tutu, an old trumpet and other items, I realized that we had identified the relics of culture. All of these items were potential interests we were exploring with our children. The ones that resonated for our children created the steps to community for them. Others became artifacts to our anthropological process for community inclusion.

Step 2: Find the Venue or Play Point

Once the change agent has identified positive capacities, the next critical step is to find the place where the person, idea or product will relate positively. Finding the setting sets the stage for inclusion and cultural shifting.

By venue or play point I am referring to the viable marketplace for the person, idea or product. With ideas or products, the change agent can think in the conventional framework of a marketplace. That is, if you have developed a product that is best suited for accountants, your potential marketplace would be the fiscal office of a corporation or with accounting firms. These or similar marketplaces offer the best possibility that your product will be understood and, hopefully, purchased.

The same thinking relates to ideas. When a novel approach is designed, the inventor is apt to be more successful if he or she shows the idea to a group or setting where the idea might best be applied. An idea, like a product, might have a wide appeal. But getting the idea initially accepted is better in a venue that relates to it.

When applying these same ideas to people, the concept of venue has equal importance. If you are looking to find a framework of new friends, you have a much better chance of connection if you take a hobby, passion or capacity and join up with others who share the same interest. A good example is the efforts we make with our children when we attempt to broaden their horizons. As I write these words I am sitting at a practice field where my youngest son, Santino, is playing football. Earlier this year he asked me if he could try football. He has been interested in the sport and follows the game. Given this interest, I began to look for a venue where Santino might test his interest and connect with others. I found such a venue with a local group called the Montour Youth Football League. In the process, Santino has developed a number of new relationships with children he has just met.

In a more formal way, this step works with agencies that attempt to connect people who have been isolated or segregated back to community. One example from my agency is the story of David. I first met David while working years ago at our local county home for the aged. Although he is not much older than I am, David had been admitted to this facility as a young man. A few years later, after I had left the county home, my new agency helped David move out of this facility to his own apartment. One of our first efforts was to help David begin to meet people and make new friends. Using the capacity model portrayed in step one, we identified a number of things that David enjoyed or had an interest in. One of David's passions is oldies music. While at the county facility, David listened regularly to oldies music on the radio. After he moved into his own apartment, we identified an oldies club not far from where he lives. This venue offered a good start point for David because he has a natural affinity for a common theme that brought others together.

In many cases, finding the appropriate venue that matches the interest or positive points of the individual is anthropological work and is critical to cultural shifting. We know that people gather for all kinds of reasons, but the most powerful is to celebrate that which they share. We covered this point in Chapter Two when we explored the common themes of cultures. In David's example, finding the oldies club was a direct match to David's interest. For Santino, it was finding the Montour Youth Football League. Often we have to look closely, but the process accelerates when we seek people who might have knowledge of the particular interest. In David's situation we called the local oldies radio station to inquire. With Santino, I saw a story in our local newspaper about the Youth Football League. The resources are there; we just have to find them.

I remember an experience that occurred while visiting Parsons, Kansas, where I had been invited to present. Parsons is a small town with maybe 12,000 people. The morning of my talk I was waiting in my motel lobby for my ride. To pass time, I looked over a brochure rack of local attractions. One brochure had caught my eye. It was a Chamber of Commerce piece that boasted about Parsons and the surrounding area. As I read the brochure, I was amazed to see that the chamber had identified over eighty clubs, groups and associations active in the Parsons area. Even this small community had people organized around over eighty areas of interest or common cause.

Another example of finding venues is the Internet. If you have been spending any time online, you know about "chat-rooms." These are settings where people gather online to explore something that they are all interested in. There is not a topic know to humankind that does not have its own "chat-room."

One caution must be addressed when applying this step of the cultural shifting process to assist the acceptance of newcomers who have been excluded. The existing members of a community may not see or understand the relevance of people who have been traditionally excluded from their midst. For example, people with disabilities historically have been separated from typical populations. Given this segregation, the natural tendency, even for professionals in human services, is to keep these same people segregated. So, if we discover a capacity (as explored in step 1) such as that our friend David loves oldies music, a natural propensity might be to see if there are other people with disabilities who like the same music and then congregate them. How many times do you see groups of people with disabilities doing the same thing together? This phenomenon is evident in our stadiums or theatres that have "handicap sections" where all people with disabilities are herded to watch the game or show, regardless of whether or not they have an accessibility need to be in a separate physical location.

Even when we find the appropriate natural community venue, the energy to segregate and congregate people still might unfold. An experience a few years back drove this home for me. I was assisting a friend of mine to connect in the community. Using step 1, I discovered that Jim had an interest in swimming. I then went to step 2 and explored Jim's community to find a swimming venue. We decided on the local YMCA near Jim's home. When Jim and I went to the YMCA to get him a membership and find out more about the swimming options, the membership director pulled me aside. In a soft voice, so that Jim wouldn't hear, he told me that he could arrange for my agency to have the pool all to us every other Tuesday evening. This way we could bring all the people with disabilities we like and they could swim together. Even the YMCA membership director thought about people with disabilities in a "congregative" manner.

The bold fact of all these experiences is that people gather. For every capacity or passion, there is a place that people gather to celebrate these passions. Once we get over our habits of segregation and congregation of those considered different in some way, we can come to see that these places offer a wonderful starting point to culture. In these gathering places we can find the key to cultural shifting and the dispensing of social capital and currency.

Step 3: Understand the Elements of Culture

In Chapter 2, we identified the key elements of community. These include:

- *Rituals*–These are the deeply embedded behaviors of the culture that the members expect others to uphold. These behaviors can be formal actions or symbolic activities that members just pick up.
- *Patterns*–The patterns of a culture refer to the movements and social space occupied by the members. Patterns are captured in how the members relate to each other as they go about the business of the culture. Patterns almost always revolve around the territory occupied by the members. As territorial

animals we are very rigid and defensive of that which we feel we have laid stake to in joining the culture.

- *Jargon*–This relates to the language, words, expressions and phrasing members of the culture use to describe or discuss that which they hold as important. Often these words might be technical or very specific to the cultural theme. Other times the jargon might manifest in sayings or expressions that are not technical, but are widely understood by other members and become important to the exchange of the culture.

- *Memory*–This refers to the collective history of the culture. The memory is honored in formal ways by producing yearbooks, annual reports and other official documents or celebrations that chronicle the actions of the culture. Other types of informal memory also happen within a culture by the weaving and telling of stories or anecdotes. Both of these approaches create a living history of the culture and establish the bond that causes members to want to continue the work of the culture. Memory leads to community wisdom.

Once people express an interest in looking further into something that excites them and discover that a culture exists, the next logical step is to understand and then carry out the actions of the culture in an effort to join. When the actions of culture get defined in these ways, it gives the newcomer clear things to consider in joining. The more they understand what the community does that is common, how they move about in doing those things, what words and phrases they use to communicate their actions and the history that bonds them, they are much more apt to become easily brought into the fold.

For cultural shifting to succeed in helping people belong to a community, first observe the community in action and be clear about your observations. These observations will help you to consider the actions needed for yourself or someone you are helping to be more easily included. The sooner you come to know the rituals, patterns, jargon and memory of the community, the quicker your passage.

The potency of this approach struck me with a computer advertisement I recently saw on TV. The ad featured a young, hip-looking fellow who was showing the features of an IBM *Think Pad* computer. Behind him was a stuffy-looking attorney. The hip fellow was telling the audience about the product and the attorney was monitoring his pitch because the company wanted to be accurate in the portrayal. As the hip fellow told about the features of the *Think Pad*, the attorney was checking his notes. The hip pitchman, after looking back to see if the attorney was paying attention, ended his pitch by saying the *Think Pad* was the "baddest" computer on the planet. The attorney jumped up and challenged him: *"You can't say that, it is not bad, it is good."* At this point in the ad the hip pitchman made a frown as if the attorney was really out of it, and the ad ended.

Obviously IBM, which is a traditional company competing in the world of forward-thinking computer users, wanted to make a statement. One was that IBM is hip and would fit in well with the nontraditional user. They used a pitchman who looked like the customers they were hoping to win. The use of the word "bad" was done to tie into the jargon of the target group they wanted to influence. Clearly IBM and the ad agency that produced the commercial had thought about the important element of jargon.

In cases where you are considering the inclusion of people you work for or care about, the process is the same. That is, the observation and analysis of the rituals, patterns, jargon and memory of the culture will help you gather the information needed to pass on to the individual you are helping. In many ways this is what we do with our children. Once we locate a possible venue for them, we gather as much information as we can to see how other members behave, move about and talk. With my son's Youth Football League I followed this script. I talked to other children and their families who played the previous year to better understand the cultural elements. This information was invaluable to me as I prepared my son for his passage into this new culture.

In situations where new ideas or products are being considered, this step is adjusted. The elements of the culture are important, but they must be framed around how the idea or product might influence or impact the rituals, patterns, jargon or memory of the culture. Indeed, new ideas or products will always change or adjust the key elements of the community. These influences must be identified and understood so as to offset challenges by the negative gatekeepers. For example, if a new computer methodology is being introduced to a group and will influence how the group does its business, the change agent needs to know this and be ready to prepare members for these changes.

Thus, with ideas or products, the change agent must do a probability analysis of the impact of the innovation on rituals, patterns, jargon and memory of the culture. One needs to remember that most people will likely be somewhat resistant to a new idea or product. The sooner the change agent can focus the impact and prepare the group for change, the easier the new idea or product will be diffused.

Either way, for people, ideas or products, understanding the elements of culture becomes a critical piece to the process of cultural shifting. The easiest way to gather this information is to observe the culture firsthand. In this observation change agents need to be open, receptive and highly observant of the cultural nuances. They need to make mental notes and, if the culture is complex, formal notes.

If observation is impossible, another way to gather information is to ask others. This type of interviewing will glean important information and perspectives from people who have had previous experiences with the culture. These leads can be invaluable. Be cautious, however, of the possibility of bias or bad information. Sometimes the informant may have an ax to grind, or may be suspicious of your questions and intentionally skew the information he or she gives.

A third method for learning the elements of community is to read. Often information for prospective members is easily at hand. The astute change agent will read as much as he or she can find on a particular community, but at the same time understands that sometimes written material can be a problem, as nuances are left out. Successful change agents will try to use all three methods. They ask, observe and read as much as they can about the community.

Step 4: Enlist the Gatekeeper

The final step in cultural shifting revolves around the gatekeeper. The only way new people, ideas or products can successfully enter an existing community is when they are introduced and endorsed by a viable gatekeeper. As we described in Chapter 2, a gatekeeper is an indigenous member of the community who has either formal or informal influence with the culture. Gatekeepers can be formally elected or selected leaders, or they might be one of the members who everyone can count on to get things done. Further, the gatekeepers can either be positive or negative, assertive or unassertive about the person, idea or product being introduced.

Gatekeepers are powerful because they transition their influence to the person, idea or product they are endorsing or rejecting. Transition of influence is the first step to the inclusion of the new thing into the culture. The mere fact that the gatekeeper likes or dislikes the idea is enough to sway some of the other members to one side. Remember, 60% of the membership of any community is usually neutral (or slightly on the negative side) on issues. Gatekeepers use their power and influence to persuade others to follow their lead. The assertive gatekeeper readily will offer an opinion, the unassertive gatekeeper usually must be asked.

To effectively shift a culture to accept something new requires that the change agent identify and then enlist a gatekeeper to facilitate the passage. This can be complex in how it plays out. On the one side we know that gatekeepers are a natural part of any culture or community. We know that generally about 20% of these gatekeepers are positive people interested in taking risks to promote things they feel good about. We know that when the gatekeeper endorses a person, idea or product, other members observe this and open their thinking to the same. Finally, we also know that the more enthusiastic the gatekeeper is to the new item, the more apt others are to do the same.

On the other hand, enlisting gatekeepers is sensitive business. The change agent needs to be aware of the manipulation factor. Most people do not want to be manipulated or be told by others what they should do. This is particularly true when the agent making the request is not a viable member of the community he or she is attempting to alter or influence. This type of "carpetbagging" is usually counter-productive to the agenda.

Still, if you want to bring a shift in cultural perspective, the endorsement and support of a gatekeeper is absolutely essential. To this end, then, the ability to identify and then ask for gatekeeper assistance without being perceived as attempting to meddle or influence is a true art in changing culture. And the process probably works differently for people than for ideas or products.

For the assertive gatekeeper, the enlistment process is usually not that difficult. These individuals are often quick to come out in support. The unassertive gatekeeper will need some prompts or requests. The level of difference the change agent is promoting will affect both the assertive and unassertive gatekeeper. That is, the more novel the item to be introduced into the culture, the less willing even assertive gatekeepers will be to sound off. Regardless of how assertive one is, if the new idea is controversial, gatekeepers will tend to be cautious for fear of rejection.

When dealing with the inclusion of new people, there are some ways all of this can be addressed to lessen the risk. For example, if a gatekeeper is identified, and then introduced to the new person attempting to be included, and they begin to "hit it off," this might signal a match. Or, if the potential gatekeeper shows an interest or propensity for someone the agent is trying to get included, this also may show a match. Further, if there is some knowledge that a person might be more approachable due to some past experience, this too might signal a match.

For instance, when working for the inclusion of people with disabilities in an existing community, if we can find a gatekeeper who has past experience with disability, or is sensitive to disability issues, he or she may be more apt to introduce the new person to the culture. In these cases, their familiarity with the point of difference gives them a much easier starting point for making an endorsement.

A good example of this was with the introduction of the Americans with Disabilities Act (ADA). When advocates were promoting the idea of a civil rights act for people with disabilities, they approached politicians who had some direct or indirect experience with disabilities to play the role of gatekeeper. One such person was Senator Tom Harkins of Iowa. Senator Harkins, who has a brother with a seizure disorder, has long been interested in disability issues. He knows firsthand how his family and especially his brother have struggled to be accepted and to be afforded their rights. Advocates for the ADA felt that if Senator Harkins could introduce the idea of a civil rights act for people with disabilities, the cause would more likely advance. Indeed it did, and the senator was a key ally and gatekeeper for the cause.

Another point of connection is if the gatekeeper had a difficult time getting into a group, he or she might be more apt to sponsor a newcomer to make things easier for the person. This sense of camaraderie is often a connection point between oppressed people. People who are successful in a culture even with their difference tend to be willing to help others who face similar discrimination. Similarly, people who perceive themselves to be liberal, or more tolerant, may have a greater openness to accept differences and endorse someone new attempting to penetrate the culture. All of these apply when the object of change revolves around people.

In attempting to promote an idea or product, the change agent might approach things differently. Certainly the gatekeeper is needed to escort the new idea into the community, but finding the right gatekeeper is key. For example, if the product is some new technology, identifying a gatekeeper who might be apt to use new technology is an obvious start. Salespeople who represent products will do well to identify viable gatekeepers to use their product around other members of the culture. As the gatekeeper demonstrates the new product in front of other members, this begins to influence the other members to request the product.

I recently saw this occur with the early hand-held computers known as Palm Pilots. This new technology offers wonderful possibilities to busy people. A known gatekeeper in a trade association that I belong to told me that a company that sells Palm Pilots gave him one to use in an effort to influence other members in our association to purchase them. His raving endorsement worked. Soon, early adopters in our group bought the devices and now most of the members carry one.

Finding and enlisting gatekeepers can be tricky business, but it is an essential ingredient for cultural shifting. Change agents must learn as much as they can about gatekeepers to enhance their effectiveness.

COMMUNITY IS LIKE A SHIP, EVERYONE OUGHT TO BE PREPARED TO TAKE THE HELM.

— HENRIK IBSEN

TURN AND FACE THE STRANGE CHANGES.

— DAVID BOWIE

CHAPTER 4
The Challenges of Change

Understanding change has been a challenge to humankind from time immemorial. One of the many reasons for the struggle is that change is a paradoxical phenomenon. On one hand it is inevitable. We are bound to change and often have no control over it. Time marches on. Minutes change to hours, hours into days and the clocks of time push us to places we may not understand and don't really want to travel to. In spite of our reluctance, we must move on. We can't stop the sands of time.

Yet, regardless of this constant perpetual motion of change, we are creatures of habit and predictability. We long to stay as we are, and once habits begin to form, it often takes heaven and earth to erase their effects. This habitual drive is very important to our sanity and security. We need things to be predictable. Too much inconsistency makes us insecure. When we are out of our habitual domain, we can become testy, nervous and unsure. Stop and think about your habitual patterns. Like me, you are probably more comfortable when you are in familiar surroundings, with things that you know and understand. When you find yourself in settings that are not familiar, you can become uncomfortable and out of sorts.

It used to be that individuals and organizations thought they could control their own destiny. The person or company predicated this on the notion that change is fully manageable and determined. This thought today is all but gone. We live in a time when our destiny is tied to many different influences, some global. Try as we might, events are often out of our control. Add to this the incredible pace of the world around us. With technology and information access changing almost daily, and with world markets and economies always unpredictable, the only constant is change.

Further, the assumption that things are predictable, and therefore manageable, also has been replaced. These realities of loss of control and the notion that things are no longer fully predictable change the way we must think about change.

The Need for Change in Human Services

A clear example of this need for change can found in human services–there are some stark examples in my own career path in services to people with disabilities. Since 1970 I have been working toward the goal of community inclusion and involvement for people with significant disabilities. All of this effort was predicated on the fact that people with disabilities were segregated from their communities, with many exiled to large and impersonal institutions. This injustice fueled me and many others and we set a course to change this reality.

In the ensuing years many programs and services were developed. Laws and public policy were changed and the march to community inclusion began. This energy was captured in the creation of group homes, sheltered workshops and other types of community living and working arrangements. Large institutions were beginning to close and it seemed we were making progress toward the goal.

Yet when one pauses to really consider the progress, not in new programs developed but in natural points of connection for people with disabilities to their communities, another reality emerges. This reality was that programs and services still kept people with disabilities apart from community. In essence, we have a dualistic reality: a separate and special community for people with disabilities in the name of special services, and a place for all the rest of community.

To me, the problem rests in how we frame the issue. If we see disability as a problem and turn attention to fixing the problem, we will continue to keep people with disabilities in separate realities. Rather, I choose to see the problem as a cultural one with macroscopic aspects that suggest a community perspective.

Of course, this analysis has not been done in isolation, and many others have suggested the same thing. Indeed, the 1980s and early '90s developed a number of perspectives and new models. An example here is the "supported employment" model. Leaders in this movement such as Paul Wehman, Tom Bellamy and Frank Rusch have suggested that we need to re-frame how people with disabilities are treated in vocational programs. A macroscopic view was suggested that introduced a "job coaching" component that would assist people in on-the-job training, rather than long-term readiness training in segregated environments.

Still, these new innovations have struggled. Some have been misunderstood, others have been mismanaged and still others have been sabotaged. As the saying goes, "Old ways die hard." This chapter is an effort to think about change from outside of the human services box. That is, rather than superimpose a human services or disability services perspective, it attempts to look at change through a larger, community lens. This broader vision of change might offer insight on how we might proceed.

Toward a Change Perspective

Although change in the world is hard to predict, certainly there are some things that can be projected to happen. Today there are many "futurists" who, using observed trends, attempt to predict what might happen in the future. For example, some futurists (Corbin, 1999) suggest that today's key changes are moving us from an information culture to one that is looking to be more spiritual and relational. This type of prediction is based upon what people and organizations that are thought to be forward thinking have said and done. Regardless, predictions are merely educated guesses.

These two realities, the unpredictable curve that drives change and the curve that resists change, produce a powerful paradox and, in turn, a tension for people and organizations. The tug-of-war that follows can derail any change effort, even a direction that is necessary for survival. Often what can happen at this juncture of the change curve is that people resist until it is usually too late.

Consider the challenge of changing a personal behavior for self-improvement. One example is the effort to change dietary patterns so you will eat better, more nutritious foods. You might cognitively understand all the elements. You know your current diet is not the best it can be. You equally know all the reasons why you should enhance your diet. All of this makes perfect sense. So you set the course for changing your diet. You decide on the foods that are better for you. You begin to stock your cabinets with these types of foods. You make a goal plan and even enter it into your daily planner. Then you begin to execute your change.

Now, all great voyages start with the first stroke of the oar, and your dietary change is no different. The first day goes fantastic. You follow your diet and clearly feel that you are on the road to change and life longevity. Even the second day is good; you're still on track. Then the third day you find yourself spontaneously invited to join some friends after work. In the course of your meeting, your friends order some nachos with sour cream. You look at this food, a favorite in your old dietary patterns, but now taboo. You pause and think, *"I've really been good up to this point, one nacho won't hurt."* So you take the biggest nacho on the dish, and scoop up a huge wad of sour cream and slowly, bite by bite, revel in the taste. Before you know it, you have single-handedly eaten a whole bowl of nachos. In a split second, the rationalization of your behavior sabotages the best-laid plans for change.

This sabotage happens not only in our personal efforts to change, but with our organizations as well. Since organizations are nothing more than a collection of individuals, the same phenomenon occurs. Like people, organizations develop habits, cultures and patterns that drive behaviors. They shape and are shaped by the people who are members of the organization.

So what do we do? Given the ongoing tension between what we want to do and our old habits, are we doomed to the status quo? The answer to this question is not simple. We are not chained to the status quo unless we want to be! We can influence the change process–but it is not easy.

A Definition of Change

An exploration on any topic mandates a definition first. So what does change mean, and how is it defined? The dictionary states that change can be a verb or noun. We can effect change or describe a type of change. As this book is about action, we'll use the definition of change as a verb from the *American Heritage Dictionary* (1992):

- to cause to be different, to transform
- to give or receive reciprocally; interchange
- to exchange for or replace with another, usually of the same kind or category

- to lay aside, abandon or leave for another; switch
- to give or receive the equivalent of money in lower denominations
- to put a fresh covering on
- to become different, transform or go from one to another
- to alter
- to become deeper in tone

Change is often thought of as going from one point to another. Clearly, it can be physical as well as mental. We can change our scene by traveling from one place to another, or change our mental model from one paradigm to another. We can change our framework or disposition from one perspective to another without moving from the spot we are in. We can change our attitude about something even if the event remains the same.

Change can be both unplanned or planned. With unplanned change the circumstances surrounding the change are outside of our control. Things happen to such an extent that the change agent has little or no influence. These unplanned situations are difficult because often the person was not planning for something new, yet he or she is forced into a new direction.

Planned change, on the other hand, is when the change agent has a degree of control or at least has influence over the decision to change. Planned change presents an opportunity for the change agent to be able to think about and to adopt some actions that might guide or influence the change into a direction the agent chooses.

There are some real definitional start points that are key to an initiation of any type of change. That is:

When we want to change.
This is when we have a desired outcome, but are not yet there. We acknowledge that something new is luring us, and the choice to act on it is ours.

When we need to change.
This is when there is some pressure to move toward the desired outcome. We either see the benefit to react to circumstances, or are being advised to make a change.

When we must change.
This is when we have no choice and the change has been forced upon us. This is mandated change and if we do not make a move, there will be serious consequences.

These three delineations not only frame the intent to change, but are key to its initiation. They help us to understand the pressure or desire for change. They also relate to the internal or external process that surrounds change. The interesting notion is that regardless of if you want, need or have to change, these elements do not necessarily make the change any easier. Even in situations where life or death might be tied to the change, people struggle mightily with the process.

For example, I think of my mother's experience trying to quit smoking. As a lifelong smoker, in an era when smoking actually was encouraged, Mom became addicted to the habit. As we children became aware of the ill effects of smoking we started to encourage her to stop. Mom is a bright lady and she knew that the reasons to stop were valid and in a real way she wanted to change this behavior, but couldn't. As a nagging cough and sore throat gave her further evidence, Mom began to recognize that she needed to change, but still struggled. Then came the doctor's demand that she must stop, or face the specter of throat cancer. This last event finally pushed her to quit.

Now this example, although it flows through the three levels from "want" to "need" to "must," has an additional element because smoking is an addictive habit and there are chemical elements working against the desired intent. Still, as we begin to explore the notion of change, we find that habitual actions, even if not chemically stimulated, are equally difficult to move beyond. In a strange way, our deeply rooted patterns are as addictive as a chemical that we have become dependent on.

The three elements of want-need-must relate to organizations and cultures as well. The organization I direct, UCP of Pittsburgh, has been through these layers a number of times. During the many strategic planning retreats I have participated in over my twenty-nine-year association with UCP, the driving force of the discussion focused on these three things. Often, in fact, we would use data, statistics or theories to drive the exact category of the change. Sometimes our philosophy of services would suggest that we want to change. Then a funding initiative would push us to say we need to change. And sometimes a law would demand that we change.

In a broader way, the same stratification happens with societies and cultures. A powerful example of this is found in the American civil rights movement. The "want" phase was driven by a moral notion that all people are equal. The "need" phase seemed to be fueled by incentives. Affirmative action and other ways to promote social/cultural change were attempted. Finally, laws and legal rulings were passed that demanded that society change. In spite of these dimensions, one might argue about how much American culture really has changed on this issue. In some cases we see civil equality, but most people would agree that we still do not have cultural equality. Gaps still exist that differentiate peoples. The culture has not fully shifted.

The Structure of Change

Mental Models

As we examine the structure of change related to cultural shifting, it is critical that we spend some time on recognizing the notion of mental models and frameworks that drive our thinking and, then, behaviors. In most everything we do, there is a mental paradigm that organizes our perspective on that matter. These models create our attitudinal constellation about life in general. Everyone has a distinct perspective on the world. This is manifested in how you feel about politics, religion, education, sports, entertainment, the arts, government and the like. To get a better perspective on this, ask the basic question, *"How do I feel about _____?"* Your answer to this question begins to establish your framework or mental model on this issue.

As basic as this seems, many people do not take the time or energy to really know their framework. In some cases they might not have thought about how they feel at all. Of course, some of these things are complex and require deep thought. Some of us resist this kind of reflection because we actually have been taught not to frame our own mental model, but to adopt those of others. For a lot of us, our perspectives on religion or politics might be that which our family provided to us. Sometimes we seemingly had no choice–we felt that was the way it always had been.

The Brazilian educator Paulo Freire contends that most of the western methods of formal education do not allow us to be more critical or analytical about these frameworks (1973, 1989). We are taught to passively sit and listen to the teacher tell us what we should believe. Then we "parrot" this information back and get our grade or gold star based on our ability to remember, rather than on an ability for critical analysis.

The American educator John Gatto (1992) further develops this notion. He contends that the educational system mechanically conditions children in a way that actually turns many of them away from education. The net effect of turning off children to education is that they do not take the time, or have the interest, to develop their own critical framework of the world.

Further, the way most of us were raised has significant consequences on how we feel–not only about things around us, but about ourselves as well. That is, our mental models of the world also are colored by our own perspectives of who we are. Psychologists call this our self-image. This is made up, in part, of the positive and negative thoughts we have about ourselves, or our self-esteem. If a people have more negative thoughts about themselves, they tend to have a poorer self-image of who they are. Conversely, if they have more positive notions, they will have a better self-image.

Some experts in self-image suggest that the typical way families raise children has more often focused on negative issues rather than positive. As discussed in Chapter 2, Shad Helmstetter (1986) compiled data that suggests that a typical child growing up in an average family in America has been told "no" or what they "could not do" more than 148,000 times before they reach their eighteenth birthday. This is a staggering statistic that sets a negative precept in personal self-esteem.

I know in my own everyday parenting I get caught in this negative cycle. Not long ago my oldest son, Dante, came home from school with his geometry test results. A policy at his school mandates that parents must sign off on tests. He set the test on the table and made a quick exit for his room. As I looked at the test results, I quickly called him back. "*Son, look at this test, you missed eight out of ten questions! You'll never get into college with these grades.*" He looked at me softly and said, "*But Dad, at least I got two right.*" My first reaction was to find his negatives, the ones he missed. I think this focus seems natural for most of us as parents. The result, however, is that this perseveration on the negative issues, in many ways, stunts positive self-image.

Although negativity leads to a poor self-image, perhaps worse is that it also leads to a negative vision of the world. Peter Senge (1990) summarized this idea of negative vision when he stated:

"*When asked what they want, many adults will say what they want to get rid of. They'd like a better job—that is, they'd like to get rid of the boring job they have. They'd like to live in a better neighborhood, or not have to worry about crime... or if their back stopped hurting. Such litanies of 'negative visions' are sadly commonplace, even among very successful people.*"

All of this is critical to change and ultimately, cultural shifting. People with positive self-images find themselves less resistant to change. These people are the ones who will take the risk that change implies. They have the inner strength to handle the unknown and to take chances. If we have a negative self-image, or the people we manage or lead have a poor self-image, the tendency will be to hang on to the status quo, rather than to try some new approach.

Consultants Ed Oakley and Ed Krug (1994) talk about an "80/20" phenomena that happens in business. Their studies have concluded that 20% of the work force will be open to change or new perspectives. The other 80% usually will resist or reject the new idea, no matter how much sense it makes. Although I am not sure if my personal experiences with employees in the human services agencies I have worked in or observed would meet this 80/20 principle, I do know that more resist than embrace. Regardless, even if the spread was less, the notion of mental models, self-image and mind-sets becomes the critical element to consider when we think about change.

The 80/20 phenomenon also occurs in the greater culture. We know that positive gatekeepers are open to new things and are willing to take risks. We also know that negative gatekeepers are reactive and resistant people. Yet it is my belief that not all of the 80% fall into the active negative gatekeeper category. The mix of informal expectations of family and the formal expectations of educational systems that focus on memory and parroting do not lead to an analytical perspective on our mental models. This can lead to negative and resistive tendencies toward change.

Another critical aspect that relates to mental models is the concept of circular flow. Change is not a phenomenon that is linear. Things go around in a circle in an organism and in an organization. Theorists who look at learning organizations capture this concept of flow. Most notable is Peter Senge in his book, *The Fifth Discipline* (1990). In this examination of learning organizations, Senge speaks to the circular notion of organizational flow by stating:

"*Resistance to change is neither capricious nor mysterious. It almost always arises from threats to traditional norms ... woven into the fabric of established power relation-*

ships… Rather than pushing harder to overcome resistance to change, artful leaders discern the source of the resistance."

Senge's point is not only relevant to the circular notions of organizations, but to the deep impact of a mental model and the embedded nature of the prevailing paradigm in communities.

Generations and Change

Another element that must be considered in the context of mental models is the generational aspect that affects the various cohorts of culture and society. There are five major generations that constitute American culture. Each of these groups has its own experiences and perspectives that have affected each group members' values and mental models. These generations are:

Pre-Baby-Boomers (pre-1945)

These are the people who grew up with a depression and world wars. They came of age at the high point of industrialization. They are highly nationalized and dedicated to loyalty. To them, security is critical, and as they came to the fore, the notion of a better future and retirement security was paramount. Though not highly educated, this generation was very thrifty and conservative. They became the strongest joiners and are deeply civic-oriented. Given the pressures of World War II, they have been called "the greatest generation."

Baby Boomers (1945-1965)

Growing up with the spoils of a devoted and loyal society, this generation was better educated and began to challenge values and assumptions. Highly career focused, their sheer numbers, some seventy-eight million, baited an intense competition. They became a very consumptive group and threw away more than they kept. Their career drive pushed them to be growth-oriented, often at the expense of their families. They were slow to marry and quick to divorce.

Generation X (1965-1976)

This group was the first to promote a sense of life balance. Time became as important as money, and although this generation focused on income, they demanded time off. A vital product of the "Gen X" group was the sports utility vehicle, which captured their lifestyle to a tee. They also were the first generation to understand and embrace diversity. They are visually oriented and extremely interactive with media. They are also the children of the divorce explosion, and the first to grow up without collective success stories from the nation (i.e., V.J. Day).

Generation Y (1977-1987)

This generation was the first to be raised with the school violence and terrorism that is now commonplace. They are technologically focused and savvy. Given their experiences, they demand authenticity and honesty. They are self-reliant and much more inclusive that all the other generations. The makeup of their world is vastly different than other generations, with dramatic changes in families, politics and institutions.

Generation Next (1988-1998)

This most recent generation, called Generation Next, will be an entirely different breed. They have been raised in the strongest economy in U.S. history. The affluence and throwaway mentality of Generation Next, however, will create a cluster of workers and leaders with a limited sense of tradition and sacrifice. These folks will be the most diverse and technologically proficient.

▲

How cultural rituals, patterns, and especially gatekeepers will influence new generations of players has great implications for how future cultures operate. Consequently, the fluidity in which future cultures incorporate new people, ideas and products is one key to cultural shifting.

The Tipping Point of Change

Another framework for understanding change is presented in Malcolm Gladwell's book, *The Tipping Point*, (2000), mentioned in Chapter 2 in the section on gatekeepers. Gladwell is a student of change and social science. He became interested in how some diseases became epidemics. He wondered if there was anything to learn from the epidemiological approach that could apply to social changes. Exploring the variables that change a medical outbreak into a full-blown epidemic, he looked closely at the people and conditions that make for a big social change. In his research he found that the "tipping point" for change is the moment of critical mass, when an idea or product becomes hot and fully disseminated in the culture. He states:

"We are all, at heart, gradualists, our expectations set by the steady passage of time. But the world of the Tipping Point is a place where the unexpected becomes the expected..."

Gladwell looks at all kinds of subtlety that can influence how people bring about change. He suggests that how people couch their words, the way they use emotion and the approach they take to others can enhance the potency of the message or product and lead it to the tipping point. So the first action to change is to get a better handle on our frameworks. Paradoxically, some of us do not really know what we think about aspects of the world, so change can be compromised from the starting gate. Or worse, we are negative and resistant to anything that is different from the status quo.

Analyzing Change

A critical start point in understanding change and cultural shifting is to analyze and understand the current reality. A good way of doing this is to consider the following three perspectives:

1. *Look at what has happened.*

   We need to view the recent past and how it has influenced what we have done personally, organizationally or on a larger scale. This implies that we are clear and honest about the way the past was and how that has given way to the current reality.

2. *Look at what is currently happening.*

   We should explore the present environment and the trends and changes that are occurring. This mandates that we are current and alert to the advances happening within our area of interest.

3. *Look at what will happen.*

   This requires that we assess how things will change. Here we need to consider the impact of technology, personnel realities and industry trends and possibilities.

All three of these points of analysis are critical to how we position ourselves when thinking about change and cultural shifting. They require that we are frank about what has happened, observant about the current advances and futuristic about what is ahead. Although these are not easy steps, they are essential in being realistic about the change process. All three elements are available to consider–we just need to dig to find out what we need to know.

Types of Change

First Order Change

There are distinct levels of change. First order change is when we realize we want or need to change, and tinker with our lives while still within the context of our current framework. For example, a boss might want to change the amount of paperwork in the office, so he or she creates an abbreviated format for staff to use. This shortened approach is better than what was before, but still requires everyone to do some paperwork. This is an example of first order change. The new format is different but still within the existing framework.

With first order change, the person or organization is making progress, but it may not be fully satisfying. In many cases, we can fool ourselves into thinking that the first order approach has solved a problem, when it has only adjusted it. This is especially true when the real problem is the framework itself. If the framework is flawed, then first order change is merely cosmetic.

An example is the use of labels in human services. Most people who work in human services would agree that labeling should be minimized or changed when it creates a negative effect. For example, it was not that long ago that people with physical disabilities were called "cripples." This term was used not only in common language, but facilities that supported people with disabilities often used this term in their title. In my own city of Pittsburgh, the facility now known as the Children's Institute used to be called The Home for Crippled Children.

As professionals became more astute about the connotations of the word "crippled," they decided to make a change. People in human services began to refer to people with disabilities as "handicapped." They soon realized that this term, too, is not acceptable. So it was changed again, this time to "the disabled." Again, some felt that this term was not appropriate, so professionals now refer to "people with disabilities."

I will be the first to admit that the term "people with disabilities" is better than the word "crippled" if you have to use a label. Yet maybe the real issue here is precisely the notion of using labels. If this is the real core of the problem, then just tinkering with the type of label is nothing more than first order change.

Second Order Change

If first order change attempts to adjust the existing framework, then second order change creates a new framework. This is where we begin to explore reformation, or even revolution. It calls for a dismantling of the old and a creation of something new. It suggests that the framework is the problem. Of course, for an individual or organization to get to this point means that they are aware and understand the framework. This is a much more complex, and to a large part, uncomfortable place, and it is critical to cultural shifting.

An example of second order change is the notion of inclusive education. Advocates for disability rights in education have called for a halt of special education and the mainstreaming of students with disabilities into regular schools. This challenge has led to powerful debates and emotional discourse. We know that segregated classes for children with disabilities not only separates them from their typical peers, but it increases stereotyping and perpetuates a myth that children with disabilities are better off in separate venues. This must change.

Yet to merely place youth with disabilities in typical schools is clearly not enough. If we truly want to create inclusion in schools, then we have to reform all of education, not just close special education programs. For inclusion to work we must change curricula, schedules, patterns and the essence of how schools operate. This is second order work, and it is incredibly challenging.

There are many reasons why second order change is difficult, but the most prevalent is that it threatens the status quo. When you suggest that something, anything, be dismantled, all of those who are still a part of the current system are put at risk. The example of educational reform offers a stark lens to look at second order change. One might make the case that we need educational reform for many reasons, over and above inclusion of students with disabilities. We know that the mechanical method of relating to children, ringing bells, parceling classes, keeping children in their seats and promoting competition over collaboration are all reasons for educational reform. We know that we do not need our children to be off from school in the summer because less and less children need to be available for farm work (the reason for a seasonal schedule in the first place).

All of this might suggest that we need educational reform. Still, we cling to an old and antiquated system; because that's the way we have always done it. The devil we know is better than the devil we do not know, and all of the other clichés we use to rationalize staying the same. In addition, there is a massive educational industry, with multi-billions of dollars invested in the historic framework, plus a teachers' union that is heavily vested in maintaining much of the status quo.

So education reformists tinker at the edges of the existing educational framework, ultimately doing little substantive change. Second order change is hard! To understand second order change is to appreciate cultural shifting. When key elements of the culture begin to embrace new things, reformation occurs. As the culture adjusts to incorporate the new person, product or idea, cultural shifting begins.

Cyclical Change

Cyclical change refers to the regular shifts of life. We talk about the seasons changing, but we know that the change will not necessarily last long, and that things will go back to the way they were. We can understand cyclical change in relation to the stock market. It goes up and down and sometimes the change can be predicted, other times not. Still, we know that there will be leveling out and corrections that make us feel somewhat balanced with the changes, even though we may not like them. With cyclical change, we need to make adjustments, but can rely on the process coming back to something we understand and can deal with.

Structural Change

Structural change occurs when events lead to a permanent change. When this happens, the basic structure of what we know has been altered and we need to adjust to the new form. Sometimes the entire framework is shattered and needs to be rebuilt or redone. Either way, the new structure will have some major differences from the replaced one. This creates a real sense of imbalance because, until the new structure gets created, everything is in chaos.

An example of structural change is when a new government is formed. In my own community this happened recently. Our county (Allegheny County, which surrounds Pittsburgh) recently replaced our board of commissioners, which had been making county decisions for the past 200 years, with a new county executive format. This has led to structural change in county decision-making.

With cultural shifting, structural change can create the backdrop, but may not lead to clear second order change. Still, structural change offers a starting point for cultural shifting and can be a good precursor to a better culture.

The Flow of Change

As we continue to consider change and cultural shifting, it is important to understand the flow of the change process. Many people think that change always happens from the outside, as a result of a decision or reason reached by others for us. Yet, change mandated from outside is not always successful. How many of us have fallen into the trap of thinking we can change people? I used to always be on a crusade to change people. I would try to change people's opinions, or attitudes, or perspectives. My older sisters always remind me that once I headed to college, not only did I become a know-it-all, but was constantly annoying in an effort to change them. It took more years than I care to admit to realize that in most regards it is usually fruitless to try to change people. Indeed, I can hardly change myself, let alone change others.

Change can happen from within or from without. Yet spouses continue to try to change each other. Bosses continue to try to change workers. Laws continue to try to change citizens. The fact is that successful change is much more of an inside-out phenomenon than outside-in. This is not to say that change is always inside-out. Certainly there are times when outside forces are so strong or compelling that difficult change can occur.

The noted consultant and author, Steven Covey (1990), explores change in much of his work. He states *"Change–real change–comes from the inside out...It comes from striking at... essential paradigms, which give definition to our character and create the lens through which we see the world."* (p. 78)

Thus, rather than try to force someone to change, it is far better to guide people to create the change themselves. When someone has an internal reason to change, there is a much greater chance that change will occur–not always, but the odds are usually better from within. This is often referred to as "ownership." When people feel an ownership to an idea, concept, vision or mission, they have a much greater commitment.

Saul Alinsky, the controversial community organizer who practiced in the Chicago area in the 1940s and 50s, had an interesting take on change. Alinsky worked to change the way poor people were treated in Chicago. Early in his career, he used to tell people that they were being mistreated and needed to push for change. This approach was rarely successful. It wasn't until Alinsky got a number of individuals to realize their plight and become personally invested that change occurred.

Alinsky (1960) also noted two basic ways that change occurred. Change from outside he called "revolution." Change from inside he termed "evolution." He wrote that both routes to change could lead to success and cultural shifting, but that there were key tradeoffs in the process. With revolution, change was always quicker but more brutal, and potentially less long-lasting. Often with revolution, once those you attempt to change get back on their feet, they strike back and try to move things to the way they were before the change. Consider political revolution. Usually these efforts are bloody and implosive. In many cases the insurgents get beaten back and thoroughly punished by the power base they attempted to replace. There are precious few examples of long-lasting revolutionary change.

Alinsky postulated that the other approach, evolution, was slower and more tedious but longer-lasting. Evolution looks to push and mold the actions of the power elite into a process of change. With evolution, the change is tied to adaptation and cultural success. This shift in the culture is powerful, but the drawback is that it is very slow. Often, before the change can really happen, those that push for it get replaced.

Alinsky depicted the issue of change by creating what he called the power triangle. At the top of the triangle are the "haves." These are the wealthy, strong or officially powerful few who hold the cards and often make the rules. These are the people who must grant or embrace the change for it to be sanctioned.

The middle level of the triangle is the "have-a-little, want-mores." These are those who represent groups, or have some vested interest in a constituency and want to see them included or welcomed. These people can be change agents or spokespersons for a cause.

The last level of the triangle Alinsky called the "have-nots." These are the largest groupings of people: those who are shut out or dis-empowered. This group is the lowest level of social stratification of the community. These are the people who get represented by those in the middle level of the power triangle.

In this schema, Alinsky suggested that the change agent could either go through the system for change (evolution) or outside the system to push a new agenda (revolution). Most change efforts I know can be analyzed in this framework.

Another legendary change agent who understood the inside-out approach was Miles Horton (1990). Throughout his career, Horton was interested in the change process. His interest led him to found the Highlander Center in New Market, Tennessee. The center has been a bastion for change over the years. In the 1930s the center helped the labor movement develop better work environments for workers. By the 1940s and 50s the center turned its attention to the civil rights movement. Rosa Parks, Ralph Abernathy, Martin Luther King and Eleanor Roosevelt were among the leaders who spent time at the Highlander Center.

Horton knew that people do not need experts to help them change. Rather, he contended, they just need a chance to think about their situation, opportunity to talk with others who are experiencing the same thing and a chance to come to some conclusions about strategies and actions. This approach is a basic empowerment of people. Horton had great confidence in the wisdom of everyday folks to figure out what they need to solve their problems. Alinsky's and Horton's perspectives on change are further elaborations of the inside and outside question. The flow of change is as vital as the reasons why we promote change in the first place.

Other experts also have talked about the various roles that people take in the change process. The key to understanding the roles of change is to appreciate how the people playing the roles relate. Conner (1992) defines four major roles as follows:

- *Sponsors*–those with the power to sanction or legitimize change. Sponsors assess dangers and opportunities, set priorities and create an environment that enables change.
- *Agents*–those responsible for actually making the change.
- *Targets*–those who actually must change and who must be educated about and involved with the change process.
- *Advocates*–those who want to achieve a change but lack the power to sanction it.

The Zones of Change

Following the thesis that inside-out change is much more potent than change that originates from the outside, we should think about working outward though three distinct zones. These zones offer us key elements for understanding and vital points for cultural shifting. The zones are:

- personal
- primary
- secondary

The Personal Zone

The most basic and foundational aspect for change is found in the characteristics related to the person attempting to change. This includes personal background, experience, habits, generational influences and exposures that have created the person you are. This includes the things you are attracted to and the things you cannot stand.

This zone is the obvious place to start for considering change. Regardless if you want, should or must change, a successful process is dependent on the ability to know and balance elements of the personal zone. Key questions to help with personal change are:

- What do I like to do?
- What don't I like to do?
- What are my "hot buttons" (things that irritate me)?
- What are my "cold buttons" (things that don't make me angry)?
- What personal aspects helped with past change efforts?
- Who might I rely on to help me?
- What is my endurance level (the time it takes to bore me)?
- What things relax me?
- How might all these ideas relate to my change?

Organizations too have a personal level. If your change goal is to have an impact on an organization or grouping of people, the personal elements also must be considered. These are found in an individual analysis of the people involved by using the same questions listed above, but related to the collective of the group. This could take some work, but is well worth the effort in giving you a better ledgehold for change. If your time is limited, you might focus attention on the formal and informal leaders of the group. Often these people, and their behavior, drive the collective actions of the group. If their behavior is accurately assessed, a solid start for change can be established.

The Primary Zone

This is the grouping of people and associations who have a close personal connection with the individual. This would include family, both nuclear and extended, friends and colleagues, as well as systems such as churches, fraternal organizations and other points of primary contact. This cluster of people around the individual are the key supporters and the core of encouragement. If these individuals or small groupings of people get behind the change, success is much more viable. Ways to identify primary players are:

- family constellation
- close personal friends

- mentors
- teachers
- clergy
- heroes

As with individuals, organizations have a primary zone as well. These include other groupings of people or players that have an allied relationship to your department or team. For example, if I am attempting to promote change with staff that provides attendant care at my organization, the primary system might be administrative support, clerical support, other agencies who do similar work, family members and the people we serve. Each of these clusters of people represents primary connectors to our attendant care staff.

The Secondary Zone

This final clustering consists of the less direct, but still influential people or systems that relate to the person considering change. The secondary zone represents the policy, procedure, history, rules or regulations, be they formal or informal, that surround the person or organization. These often are the confines of the way things are and have a deep impact on the way things might evolve. A laundry list of secondary things to consider is:

- formal structure
- current resources
- laws
- policy
- procedure
- current paradigms
- government structures
- regulations
- bylaws
- current informal trends
- current knowledge

Organizations have had a historical focus on these secondary issues. Given the industrial roots and mechanistic tendencies of most organizations, the secondary issues of policies and procedures have reigned supreme. To this end, most companies have felt that if they created a rule or regulation, this would guide the change. Today we know that change is a phenomenon that most effectively happens from the inside-out.

Another way to understand these zones of change is to think about their points of assimilation. One way to do this is to consider the following three perspectives:

- *Micro Change*–the change and shifting that affects you, your spouse, family, close friends and associates. This relates to when "I" have to change.
- *Organizational Change*–the change affects the primary organizations in your life, your company, church, clubs, groups and associations. This relates to when "we" have to change.
- *Macro Change*–acknowledges the broader, cultural systems. Included here are national, international and global aspects that impact change. This relates to when "everyone" must change.

Although cultural shifting is implicit in all three perspectives, the notion of organizational change is more about how the culture is impacted. Conner (1992) suggests that control and the ability to assimilate change is key. He notes that control is *"what we all seek in our lives, and the ambiguity caused by the disruption of expectation is what we all fear and avoid."* In order to successfully change, we must be able to *"assimilate change at a speed commensurate with the pace of the events taking place…,"* while understanding the micro implications of organizational or macro change. (p. 85)

The Change Curve

Still another perspective on the flow of change comes from the business concept of the change curve. Most business ventures move through three major changes. The first is the phase of *entrepreneurial action*. This is the period when an idea is launched and there is great excitement. The leaders are innovators and new paradigms are being created. For many people this is a highly charged period where dreams begin to be realized.

Once the idea is launched and the product or service is being sought, the second phase begins—that of *growth and development*. In this period, great strides are made as more and more demand for the product or service meets with production and rapid growth. Protocols for development get detailed, and to a certain extent, entrenched.

As the product or service hits a peak, the natural tendency is for the *decline or renewal* to set in. The product or service is now widespread and other competitors probably have entered the field. The organization might decline unless it can find ways for renewal. Experts in organizational change often will focus attention and action on the ways that renewal can occur. These three phases have been articulated by Lynch and Kordis (1988), and are summarized nicely by Ed Oakley and Doug Krug in their thoughtful book, *Enlightened Leadership: Getting to the Heart of Change* (1994).

Anyone who has worked for an organization or for some type of social cause can relate to these three phases. New things often are embraced and are cause for excitement to those who can see the benefit. Yet the growth and late growth phases are ones we have all experienced. The real challenge for success of individual and organizational change is to move from the growth phase to renewal of our vision. We can move from the status quo to something new, but it isn't easy.

Resistance to Change

It is clear that change is not easy. As creatures of habit, it is never simple for us to go from one set of behaviors to a new one. As we continue this exploration of change, we would be remiss if we did not dissect the key resistances to change. Resistance can occur much more aggressively with negative gatekeepers, and often with neutral members of culture. Although resistance is present for everyone, the positive gatekeepers have fewer problems with these issues. Liebler and McConnel (1999) offered perspectives on resistance, including:

Lack of trust

People do not trust the reasons, strategy or agent leading the change effort. Again, this notion of trust is a key element to change.

Different assessment of the situation

The team sees the situation differently than the decision-maker or change agent does. This often happens when the team feels less invested in the situation than the leadership. The change agent must figure out ways to get the team invested.

Desire to protect the status quo

The team wants to keep things the way they have always been.

Protection of self-interest

The team sees no benefit to themselves. Change means that people need to learn new things. Going back to being an apprentice is a strong deterrent to change.

Schermerhorn and his associates (2000) identified other major ways people will resist change. These are:

Fear of the unknown

It is natural for people to fear what is not known. This unknown can create a formidable obstacle, especially for negative gatekeepers who are looking for the easiest reason not to change.

Lack of good information

Sometimes the change agent does not bring forward good information to those intended to follow the change, and this lack of information creates resistance.

Fear of loss of security

A new direction suggests that the existing direction is stale. This can create insecurity in people. People will go to heroic efforts to avoid insecurity. These efforts lead to staying the course rather than embracing something new.

No reasons to change

When people do not see or know viable reasons why they should change, they will tend to maintain the status quo.

Fear for loss of power

People do no like to be rendered irrelevant, or feel they lack a skill. Yet, a new direction makes everyone an apprentice. The loss of power is a potent deterrent to change.

Lack of resources

Even if people see the wisdom or need for change, they can be resistant if they feel they do not have the resources or tools. The positive gatekeeper needs to assure them that other people, especially those neutral members of the community, have the resources to change.

Bad timing

Regardless of the viability of the change, if the timing is not right, resistance can happen. Many a good idea has failed because it was introduced at the wrong time.

Habit

Many people know they should adjust or change, and really want to, but the habits of the old ways can create a formidable obstacle and lead to resistance. Negative gatekeepers tend to be people who are more easily habituated to their present situation.

Resistance can come in overt or covert ways. Sometimes it is clear that people are resistant and other times people are more cloaked in how they resist. Both types are difficult to deal with, but covert change, or sabotage, can blindside the change agent. Regardless, resistance also can manifest around one or all of three points. These are:

- *Resistance to the change*–people feel that the need to change is not viable and they have no vested interest to follow.
- *Resistance to the change strategy*–centers on how the change is being perceived.
- *Resistance to the change agent*–the team can understand the reasons as well as the strategy, but have a problem with the person leading the change. This resistance can pertain to the positive gatekeeper as well.

As we explored earlier, all groups, teams or communities have both positive and negative gatekeepers. It is often the negative gatekeeper who leads the resistance or directly sabotages the change approach. Conversely, resistance to change can be mitigated by the affirmation of the positive gatekeeper. The wise change agent will look for cultural support. In this regard, the positive gatekeeper lessens resistance to the change agent by promoting the process of cultural shifting.

Vision and Change

Leading experts in organizational change all acknowledge vision as one of the first critical notions of promoting change. John Kotter, in his book, *Leading Change* (1996), states, *"Vision…motivates people to take action in the right direction, even if the initial steps are personally painful."* (p. 68)

Vision offers a start point for anything new. If you want to go from point A to point B, having a vision that charts your course is essential. Maps, for example, establish vision for movement in travel. It seems to be the most foundational of concepts to change. Peter Block (1987) offered the following definition of vision. *"Vision is our deepest expression of what we want. It is…an ideal state…It expresses the spiritual and idealistic side of our nature. It is a dream created in our waking hours of how we would like our lives to be."* (p. 52)

For organizational purposes, vision differs from mission. The mission statement of an organization identifies what it does. The vision statement identifies why it does it. At my organization, for example, our mission speaks to the kinds of services we offer to individuals and families that experience disability. Our vision statement, which is *"building a community where each belongs"* articulates why we do what we do. In our case, the mission-oriented actions set the tone for preparation and action so that people with disabilities can be active in community. This involvement in community helps create a place where all people have a role and are valued.

The most successful groups on the change curve are those that can align their mission with their vision. The notion of alignment helps to promote a focus that is essential to organizational and individual change. According to Oakley and Krug (1994), *"Vision…brings out the best in ourselves and in our organizations."* (p. 172)

Vision can be further defined as the capacity to frame a direction in taking action on a cause. Often vision can be displayed by using a before-and-after poster. Many advertisers use this method to create a vision for a product that will bait the consumer to make a purchase. Weight loss programs for this method are legion. These graphic illustrations of how things might be if we join a diet program or buy a diet suppressant are very convincing.

TV, magazine and poster ads are everywhere touting the success of Rogaine, the hair growth drug. As baby boomers age and begin to lose their hair, Rogaine has become in great demand. Yet, all these ads really do is create a vision for action. The action, of course, is to have consumers purchase the product.

To create a vision does not always require a visual image. Slogans, titles, names and other words and sounds conjure up mental images that can drive behaviors. We know that product or company tag lines can build a vision. Think of the many slogans designed to promote actions on the part of the consumer.

- We do things right™
- Just do it™
- Once you pop, you can't stop™
- Working at the speed of business™
- Feel the power™
- We try harder™
- Have it your way™

Organization mission statements offer a segue to a vision. Many companies pay top dollar to advertising and marketing firms to help frame a vision statement that creates energy. Another method of pushing a vision, however, is organization logos. A logo is a simple picture, illustration or portrayal that captures the organization's thrust. Again, the business of helping produce logos, or to enhance a visual, is competitive and expensive.

These ideas of logos and slogans often are designed to produce a company "brand identity." The idea of a brand identity is when the product name becomes synony-

mous with the product's industry. For example, the name "Levis" has been so promi-
nently associated with blue jeans that the two items are almost interchangeable.
The same is true with Xerox. You can routinely hear people ask for a Xerox copy.

Another median to create a vision is through music. In the world of advertising, product songs, jingles and other types of music can create such a powerful
mood that a vision can be developed. Anthems, school fight songs, military marches
and the like all create a vision of winning. Musical scores that accompany movies
are essential to establishing the mood that supports the plot and action.

Another vital role driven by vision is the "tension" it causes. Once a person or
organization has a vision of where they want to be, it becomes obvious that this is
not where they currently are. The gap causes tension. This might cause the person
or organization to give up on the vision, or it might push the person or entity
toward a creative action to get closer to the vision. Peter Senge (1990) refers to
this action as follows:

*"The juxtaposition of vision (what we want) and a clear picture of the current reality
(where we are relative to what we want) generates…'creative tension': a force to bring
them together, caused by the natural tendency of tension to seek resolution."* (p. 142)

If a person's vision is impaired in some way, the vitality of change can be affected. What we see is dependent on what we are prepared to see. If the vision is
too far-reaching from the current reality, the distance may lead to a failure to change
far enough. This is why strategic planning efforts always start with a thorough analysis
of the internal and external environments.

At the agency where I work, United Cerebral Palsy (UCP) of Pittsburgh, as
with most rehabilitation agencies, the framework for vision was based on a medical
model. Most of our early programs were structured from the perspective of helping
an individual fix the deficit or enhance functionality. To do this we felt we needed
to assess the individual's problems. Given this paradigm, all of our early strategic
planning and program action was tied to this premise.

In the course of my work, however, two themes began to change my thinking.
One was the fact that UCP couldn't really help fix disability deficits. We could not
make people with significant disabilities become significantly different than they
were. As much as we wanted to help people become vital parts of the community,
to attempt to change people with disabilities through the use of a classic medical
model did not produce this result. Concurrent with this reality was a changing
world where people with disabilities were becoming more militant and frustrated
with how they were perceived and treated by rehabilitation organizations. The
civil rights effort was drifting into the era of disability rights.

Both of these growing perspectives were uncomfortable for us. Our intent was
good, but our outcomes were missing the mark. This frustration began to push us to
challenge our framework. Initially this was difficult. My first reaction was not to see
the framework as the problem. We just do not want to admit that, as the cartoon
character Pogo once said, *"I have met the enemy and he is us."* Yet this reality became
more and more clear. Once we got to this point, no matter how painful, we were
ready to craft a new vision.

▲

This chapter has taken a broad-based look at change that suggests clear ramifications for human services. If we remind ourselves of the goals of community inclusion and quality of life we have crafted for our agencies and human services in general, the first key question revolves around why we have not achieved that goal for so many people. Our struggle to realize change also must be considered within the context of those we are trying to influence. By considering the generational realities of our emerging work force, we can garner helpful clues to promote change.

WHEN WE TRY TO BRING ABOUT CHANGE IN OUR SOCIETIES, WE ARE TREATED FIRST WITH INDIFFERENCE, THEN WITH RIDICULE, THEN WITH OPPRESSION. AND FINALLY, THE GREATEST CHALLENGE IS THROWN AT US; WE ARE TREATED WITH RESPECT. THIS IS THE MOST DANGEROUS STAGE.
— A. T. ARIYATRATNE

MANY OF LIFE'S CIRCUMSTANCES ARE CREATED BY THREE BASIC CHOICES: THE DISCIPLINES YOU KEEP, THE PEOPLE YOU CHOOSE TO BE WITH AND THE LAWS YOU CHOOSE TO OBEY.

— C. MILLHOFF

CHAPTER 5
Framework for Change

Cultural shifting is a process. Regardless of the significance of clear component events, change happens in a flow. To be in front of change, or to manage it, requires us to think about change frameworks. A framework attempts to capture the key benchmarks in an issue. This allows us to isolate certain variables in an effort to build a better understanding of the process.

Perhaps one of the first theorists to explore the social elements of change and postulate a framework was Kurt Lewin (1958). As a social psychologist, Lewin was intrigued by the notion of change and its impact on people and systems. Although others had written and studied change prior to him, Lewin introduced a type of framework that provides a starting point in thinking about change. He suggested the following three perspectives:

- The *present* state identifies the current reality, the status quo. When thinking about the present state we look at what is happening around us as we get ready to initiate the actions for change.
- The *transition* state is the impact of the change as we attempt to alter the course of the current reality.
- The *desired* state is the projected result and outcome you hope for, given the impact of the change. In the desired, state Lewin suggests we focus on the goal.

Lewin's framework can be considered for both personal and organizational issues. For example, if your present personal state is that you want to lower your blood pressure and weight, then the desired state is to target a goal for your weight and blood pressure. This frames where you want to be after the change. The transitional state is a zone of tension between the present state and the desired outcome. In this state you are challenged with the tension of a diet and exercise regime.

The transitional state is the key piece in Lewin's framework. This is when the mettle of the person or organization is tested. Often, if the desired state is too far off or too great of a goal, the tension brought on during the transitional state may be too much. Many people and groups fail at this point.

Individual Change Frameworks

For individuals, one might consider a decision-making framework in which to analyze change. For example, when a situation occurs that you want, need or must change, you are at the point of deciding to do something different. Typical steps to a decision-making process would be:

- Accepting the decision to change.
- Reviewing all the possible options that might lead to the desired outcome.
- Rating all the options to see which one fits best for the change you want to make (of course, you must be as honest with yourself in identifying the best course).
- Selecting the best option and gearing up to put it into play.
- Evaluating the effectiveness of the strategy by using objective benchmarks.
- Making changes or adjustments to your strategy based upon your objective evaluation.

This framework, or variations of it, is often used to help manage or promote individual change in behavior or actions. More often than not, most of us might not be fully cognizant that we are following a framework, but indeed we do. And this process, if we are able to actually focus on it, can lead to a more desirable outcome.

Organizational Change Frameworks

Groups of people who want, need or must change also are inclined to be more successful by following change frameworks. In fact, some experts argue that frameworks are a must for an organization to change and for cultural shifting to occur. To this end, many theorists have developed frameworks for change. It is prudent for us to consider some of these thoughts.

Conner's Framework of the Stages of Change

Daryl Conner offers one approach to understanding change. In his book, *Managing at the Speed of Change* (1992), Conner uses the loss-grief work of Elisabeth Kubler-Ross and offers the following eight stages related to change:

- *Phase I–Stability*: The status quo that precedes the announcement of the change.
- *Phase II–Immobilization*: The initial reaction to a negatively perceived change is shock, temporary confusion or complete disorientation.
- *Phase III–Denial*: This is characterized by an inability to assimilate new information, causing it to be rejected or ignored.
- *Phase IV–Anger*: This is evidenced by frustration and hurt, as people lash out, sometimes at those close by, who also are usually the ones most willing to be supportive.
- *Phase V–Bargaining*: People begin negotiating to avoid the negative impact of change, as people realize it cannot be avoided, marking the beginning of acceptance.

- *Phase VI–Depression*: This is a normal response to negatively perceived change, and includes resignation to failure, feeling victimized, a lack of emotional and physical energy and disengagement from one's work. Depression can represent a positive step in the acceptance process as the change is finally acknowledged.
- *Phase VII–Testing*: In this stage, people begin regaining a sense of control by exploring ways to redefine goals.
- *Phase VIII–Acceptance*: Acceptance is not the same as liking it. It just means that the individual is realistic and more productive. (pp. 132-135)

Kotter's Eight-Stage Process of Change

John Kotter, professor of leadership at the Harvard Business School, also has been a proponent of an eight-stage process of creating major change (1996). He states: "*Needed change can still stall because of inwardly focused cultures, paralyzing bureaucracy, parochial politics, a low level of trust, lack of teamwork, arrogant attitudes, a lack of leadership in middle management, and the general human fear of the unknown. To be effective, a method … must address these barriers and address them well.*" (p. 20)

- Establishing a sense of urgency.
- Creating the guiding coalition.
- Developing a vision and strategy.
- Communicating the change vision.
- Empowering broad-based action.
- Generating short-term wins.
- Consolidating gains and producing more change.
- Anchoring new approaches in the culture.

Kotter's stages offer a flow chart to organizational change. As most organizations, like people, become comfortable with the way things are, he suggests that the first four steps help to defrost the hardened status quo. This sets the organization up for change. The next three steps introduce the new ideas or suggestions. The last step attempts to strengthen the new idea into the existing culture. This step acknowledges the notion of cultural shifting.

Rosen's Principles for Change

Robert Rosen (1996) offered still another eight-part framework for change. Rosen, a psychologist and management consultant, suggests key principles associated with leadership and organizational change:

- *Vision*: Leaders see the whole picture and articulate that perspective to create a common purpose that mobilizes people into a single, coherent enterprise.
- *Trust*: Trust binds people together, creating a strong, resilient organization. To build trust, leaders are predictable, and they share information and power.
- *Participation*: The energy of an organization is the participation and efforts of its people. The leader's challenge is to unleash and focus this energy, inspiring people at every level of the enterprise to pitch in.

- *Learning*: Organizations must promote constant innovation, and the leaders must encourage their people to refresh their skills and renew their spirits.
- *Diversity*: Successful leaders understand their own biases, and they actively cultivate an appreciation of the positive aspects of people's differences.
- *Creativity*: Leaders pay close attention to people's talents, leaning on their strengths and managing around their weaknesses. They encourage independent, challenging thinking.
- *Integrity*: Every wise leader has a moral compass, a sense of right and wrong. Good leaders understand that good ethics is good business.
- *Community*: A mature leader stresses the organization's responsibility to the surrounding society. (pp. 21-22).

Krause's SPARKLE Approach on Leading Change

Donald Krause (1997) designed another interesting framework for change that uses a catchy acronym, SPARKLE. These notions apply the principles of Sun Tzu and Confucius to the change process:

- *Self-Discipline*: A leader tends to live by a set of rules or principles appropriate for him or her and acceptable to one's constituents. A leader does not need external motivation to ensure performance.
- *Purpose*: A leader develops intense determination to achieve one's vision and objectives. This creates high morale and spirit among constituents that allows the leader to effectively employ both personal and organizational power to accomplish goals.
- *Accomplishment*: A leader defines results in terms of meeting the needs of one's constituents. Taking effective action is the basis for successful results.
- *Responsibility*: A true leader owns up to the results of his or her decisions and actions and shares their consequences. The most critical of a leader's duties is an overriding concern for the best interests of his or her constituents.
- *Knowledge*: Knowledge has three aspects. The first, fundamental knowledge, deals with studying science, history and human nature. Strategic knowledge concerns understanding the needs and goals of both constituents and competitors and planning effective operations to reach objectives. Tactical knowledge focuses on uncovering evolving threats and opportunities and responding swiftly and appropriately to them.
- *Leadership*: A leader understands the special nature of the social and moral contract between leaders and their constituents and must work cooperatively with others to reach agreed-upon objectives.
- *Example*: A leader's actions become a model for the actions of one's constituents and sets a moral tone. In all situations, the leader demonstrates preferred behavior by his or her actions.

▲

To a greater or lesser degree, successful organizations follow these kinds of frameworks. If we truly want to change a system, we must think through the flow of the change. To this end, then, I would like to offer my own framework for change that can apply to either organizations or individuals. This process is one that I have been developing over the many years I have been a change agent. Although it has guided more formal efforts for change, I have found it equally effective with social and cultural change efforts as well. More importantly, this process seems to lay a solid groundwork for cultural shifting.

A Framework for Broad-Based Change

Any framework or process seems to work best when people understand it and can remember to put it into play. To this extent, the framework I have developed and want you to consider follows a basic process. To help remember the flow, all the words start with the letter "P." An overview of this framework is found in the following figure.

Broad-Based Change Framework

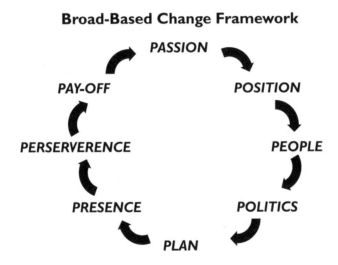

Passion

All meaningful change starts with a passion to do something different. I use the word passion because it is a strong term, one that arouses emotion. The origin of the word is Latin for suffering. Many references to the word passion flow into religious literature that explores the death of Jesus Christ. More current interpretations of passion relate to lust and fiery emotions. The dictionary defines passion as:
- A powerful emotion such as love, joy, hatred, or anger.
- Ardent love, strong sexual desire, lust.
- Boundless enthusiasm.
- Abandoned displays of emotion, especially anger.
- The suffering of Jesus.

The power denoted in the word passion is a strong starting point for change. Remember that just getting ready to change is hard work. Most of us are content where we are, even if we are pushed to change. The status quo of habits and in-grained rituals is hard to overcome when we are exposed to new ways of doing things. If given the chance, most people will stay where they are, rather than move to a new place. Thus, we use the word passion. If we are to change, we must have a deep reason to move from what is known to the unknown.

Most scholars who have looked at change, especially broad and meaningful change, recognize passion as a key ingredient. The United States civil rights move-ment was born from passion. The notion that people were treated in hostile, de-valuing ways caused a deep and compelling passion for justice and equality. People of all walks of life, all colors and ages, were drawn to the goal of civil rights. If fact, the passions were fueled by scripture and song that called people to do the hard work of change. The passions of deep homilies and loud prayers continued to offer the strength to combat the inequities and abuses that were commonplace in a seg-regated society.

Similarly, the antiapartheid actions in South Africa used the power of passion over many years to promote change. The unbelievable fact that Nelson Mandela endured more than twenty-seven years in prison and then rose to the presidency of his country is the stuff of raw passion.

Stories near and far follow the same route. From dramatic to mundane, any type of powerful change you can think of is rooted in passion. You probably know people who have passionately followed their hearts or dreams and have created a major change in their lives. I remember as a college sophomore taking a class titled "Dynamic Thinking." The essence of the class was that anything a student wanted or hoped for was achievable if passions drove them. At that time I felt that the course was mostly hype and that there might be things that a student could hope for that were totally out of the realm of possibility. So the class baited the teacher with ideas that seemed preposterous, like making millions of dollars or running for a high political office. His simple response was that any of these things could hap-pen, if we wanted it passionately enough.

As I reflect on this now, I understand the wisdom of this course, and believe my "Dynamic Thinking" professor was right. Most of the things I am truly passionate about I have achieved. However, passion is not without its sacrifices. Indeed, the most common Judeo-Christian understanding of passion is within the context of the passion of Christ. This, of course, refers to the deepest sacrifice made, that of the death of Christ. All powerful stories of change, fact or fiction, are deeply woven with sacrifices made on behalf of the change.

Position

All change suggests a position. This is manifested in what the change is about. After all, what is change but simply the movement from one place or position to another? A critical ingredient to this is the nature of the anticipated position. Po-sition is where you want to be, or what you stand for. People often ask each other, *"What is your position?"* on a particular issue. This question sets the tone for change.

In the context of this analysis, position is best understood as where you want to be or what you want to change to. The position of the civil rights movement was full equality and rights for all citizens. This is what advocates stood for and worked toward. The position for a particular company might be to acquire an additional 10% of the market share for its product. This would represent a goal or objective for the company. A position for a person might be to get in better shape, or to lose weight. This is your desired state or outcome.

In this scheme of things, regardless of your position, if your passion is intact you will find success that much closer. By the same token if you are not successful in achieving your position, perhaps you did not want it badly enough.

Another part of positioning is to consider the sub-positions that might be relevant to your ultimate goal. That is, you might set a position for yourself, but that position is dependent on the successful achievement of a sub-position. An example might be found with the personal position of losing weight. When you think closely about your position, it might mandate that you are able to put the building blocks of exercise and diet in place to support your ultimate position.

Your position, to continue to develop your passion, must be simple and succinct in how it is developed. If your position is too difficult to describe or define to others, then it will be hard not only to stay passionate, but to keep focused. Many great positions were not achieved because they were much too complex in their development. The ultimate position might be complex, but the sub-positions must be easily definable.

In some ways, position is a type of vision, but tends to be much more clearly stated and focused. Sometimes the position is defined for you, and other times you define and set the position. Position gives you something to shoot for, but is not as broad and sweeping as visions often are. Regardless, all positions that you articulate to fuel your passion must be effectively communicated to other people who are allied or essential to the position. This brings us to the next element–people.

People

"*No man is an island*" is a famous statement and, as it relates to change, clearly is true. Change almost always requires other people to assist, facilitate, cooperate or participate. Solo efforts usually lead to failure to obtain your position. In the exploration of the people factor of change, no allies should be overlooked. Change is hard enough, but if you build other people into your plan, you stand a greater chance for success. This applies to all aspects of change.

All management and leadership gurus talk or write about the people factor of organizational success. The most successful leaders always have a propensity for building other people into their plans. Stop and think about any efforts you have previously addressed and consider the people factor. I know for myself, when I have been most successful or have had an easier time with change, it is because I have connected with people who shared my passion and position.

In fact, all of us have the ability to choose those people we want to associate with. Aside from relatives, most of the other people assembled in our lives are those we have chosen. Even with our relatives, we can artfully dodge them when situations demand and no one chains us to our families. Most people make selections about people connections every day. As it relates to change and achieving our positions, we must choose wisely.

This is vital to change because the social networks we establish easily influence us. Psychologists refer to this phenomenon as a social influence theory that describes how our peer networks directly or indirectly influence our behaviors. In fact, given this social influence theory, it is amazing that most of us are alive and well at this moment. Just think about all the not very smart or risky things you did as a kid because everyone else was doing or recommending the behavior. I remember my mother (in fact, I think this is true of all mothers) saying to me: "*Are you going to jump off a bridge just because your friend has?*" Our moms had an inherent understanding of the social influence theory. My mom was always trying to tell me whom I should or should not keep as friends. Now, all these many years later, I know my mother was right. Change and behavior is deeply connected to the people you assemble around you. Thus we must choose wisely.

Think now of the people you select to mentor a new staff member. The new worker is excited about getting the job and cannot wait to show what he or she can do. If the mentor is a skeptic, this attitude will be conveyed to the new staff member. If the mentor is negative toward the director or the organization, the new worker will probably fall prey to this attitude. Conversely, if a mentor is enthusiastic or positive about the company, its mission or your position, this positive attitude will spread to the new worker.

So my advice is to think this through and choose wisely. If you associate with whiners and moaners, you will begin to whine and moan yourself. Select people who ignite you, who challenge you to do better, to reach beyond your grasp. These people will keep you going and fuel your passion. And remember how important passion is to your successful change.

Plan

Once people of like mind begin to connect, plans are made. These plans usually revolve around the issues or notions that the people have in common. The planning process is the identification, plotting and focus of the common concern into a direction that can be understood and measured. Planning can happen on an individual as well as a group basis. Planning follows some basic steps. These are:

1. Identification of issue of concern and ability to communicate it in a way that people understand and can join in.
2. The identification of the goal or outcome that might address the concern.
3. A detailed analysis of the variables and factors that affect the concern.
4. An identification of the people, products or things necessary to carry out the plans.
5. Clarification of the steps and stages necessary to reach the goal.
6. A focus of which steps come when in the process.
7. The initiation of the first step.
8. An ongoing analysis and evaluation of how the steps are moving along.

This process happens in every effort for change. A good example to illustrate these steps was an experience I had in Pennsylvania a number of years ago.

Step one: People passionate about disability issues had come together for a governor's conference in our state. At the gathering we spent time trying to identify the issues where there was common ground for the myriad of people attending the conference. By using a goal planning process we identified the isolation and institutionalization of people with disabilities as a key area to address.

Step two: After we had agreement on this, the next step was to ask, *"What can we do about this?"* Although there were differences of opinion on goals and actions, the notion of developing a statewide attendant care program became increasingly accepted. It was one service that seemed to cross the disability boundaries and offered one tangible solution to help alleviate the problem.

Step three: Once agreement was garnered for a statewide attendant care program, the data collection period began. We needed to know how many people with disabilities in the state needed attendant care. We needed to know how many people had private attendant care. We needed to know how many people were in institutions unnecessarily because attendant care did not exist. We needed to know how many states already had attendant care programs. We needed to know how much it would cost to provide attendant care to our state citizens with disabilities. All of this data needed to be gathered.

Step four: Next we began to assemble the information we gathered and focus the resources necessary to construct a true plan. We needed to identify the people in state government, elected and appointed, who might be able to help us navigate the bureaucracy. We needed economic analysis in an effort to make a fiscal case.

Step five: Now the stepping stones to change were ready to be laid. We began to craft and chart all the stages necessary to change. We needed to get written material circulated that identified and articulated our plans and we needed to solicit letters of support.

Step six: We organized the order of things to be done. First was to mobilize our key legislator to begin to draft the bill to build the attendant care program from. Next we contacted the other key legislators, in a nonpartisan fashion, to support the effort. Then we launched our effort.

Step seven: Once organized, we made the first step by having our representative submit the bill for consideration. This action had us off and running.

Step eight: All along in the process we were keeping track of our efforts and successes. We were well-organized and knew that communications, deadlines and celebrations were critical to the process.

▲

The net result of this effort was an attendant care bill that was passed by the legislature and signed into law by our governor. The plan had worked and we were now ready for the really difficult work of carrying out the program. As I reminisce on this process, I think it was successful because of three key actions:

1. *Unification*: The group was unified about the concern and the solution. This creates a powerful solidarity and starting point for change. Often, people can't agree on the problem, let alone the solution. In our situation the agreement on the issue of attendant care really energized the group.

2. *Adequate Resources*: We were able to garner financial support through a funding source, the Pennsylvania Developmental Disabilities Council, that gave us the resources to meet, communicate and underwrite a point person to lead the effort. This notion of resources cannot be understated. As much as we would like to think that passion for something will drive it forward, having the needed resources is always at the core of any major success.

3. *A Viable Point Person*: Once a point person was identified, his job was to keep us focused and to actualize our plans. Given the fact that our effort was statewide, communication was critical. Our point person kept us mobilized and on task in this process. People are busy and they can be diverted easily to other tasks. Having some way to keep people centered on task is critical to leading change.

So, planning offers the structure for change and establishes the parameters in which the direction is set and measured. The planning process creates the tone for cultural shifting. The notion of managing people toward the plan leads us to the next major step in the framework–that of politics.

Politics

Any time people assemble for a goal or action, politics come into play. By the word politics I am referring to the basic human interactions and the things that influence us. Although the word politics often is associated with governments and elections, the notion of politics is really about relationships. Even in the governmental sense, politics is essentially the alliances and positional relationships that lead to the election or enactment of people or policies. Yet none of this can happen unless people assemble and agree on something. This alignment is critical to any change effort. As we think about achieving a position, we must consider politics.

In the broad sense of organizational change, politics are essential. A few years ago my organization considered making a change in its basic direction and actions. We wanted to move from being a disability-specific services provider to a broader notion of supporting community issues. In this process, it was essential that key board members, staff and families understood and supported our direction. To achieve this I had to invest a good deal of time to explain, answer questions and enlist others to understand and support this change. The driving action to this effort was the political process. Key stakeholders had to be supportive until actions could be clearly adjusted toward our new objective.

Even with personal change, other people play a key role and the method of alignment is a political process. You need to have people be supportive of your position. This means you must clearly communicate with others. Indeed, with organizational or personal change, politics is driven by communication. If things work or do not work toward your cause, you can bet communication (or lack of it) is the reason.

Another element of politics is the bargaining process. This is about giving something in order to get something. Most of us learn this simple element of human engagement early in our lives, but today there seems to be so much more of the *"what's in it for me"* mentality. Good politicians understand this and even though they may not like it, can play the game to get to the end product.

Even with individual goals or plans for change, this type of bargaining can happen. I remember having this very struggle when I was working on my doctorate, an individual goal I had set for myself. Once I completed my classroom work, the independent study phase began. This is when the bargaining started for me. The classroom work seemed easy because I had professors setting the bar and holding me accountable. It is the classic case of someone knowing what is best for you. When I reached the independent study phase, the game changed. I am a driven person, but I have to admit that I debated with myself many times in this phase about continuing on. I used every excuse imaginable: *"I am getting too old," "What difference will a Ph.D. make," "There are so many other important things I could be doing with my time," "I can always come back to this later," "I've proven I can do the work,"* and so on.

This roller coaster went up and down all during my research. Thank goodness that I could make the best of the high times and move my work forward. In some ways this is being self-political. It calls us to find the ways we can encourage ourselves toward the change we are hoping for. Whether you are trying to lose weight, learn a new task, stop smoking or become more productive with your time, the greatest enemy to your success is yourself.

Presence

Once the change process has begun, the critical element now turns toward you. That is, change won't happen unless you make it happen. Any change that is worth its salt will not happen because you wish it to. You can be concerned or angry or annoyed or worried, but your plight will remain the same until you do something about it. Quite simply, you have to be present to make change happen.

As simple as this seems, it is amazing to me how many folks drop the ball at this point. If you want to get a promotion at work, or make the team or become published, you must drive the goal home. You need to do the work necessary to get the change you want. A healthier body means hours at the gym or the exercise mat. A bill passed in your state legislature requires that you take the time to lobby for the bill. A job promotion means putting in the time and energy to be noticed and be prepared for the assignment you would like to have. All of this takes time.

The saying: *"An overnight success usually takes fifteen years"* isn't an overstatement. Look at any role models you might hold up as a mentors or heros. The status they have achieved did not just happen. They made it happen. Unfortunately, in our culture, children are led to believe that things happen by immediate osmosis.

Our instant gratification society causes people to think that good things will magically come to them. Certainly there is magic, but it is found in hard work and presence.

Often in talking about this with my children, I remind them of an adage I read years ago in a book by Woody Allen. He said that 90% of success is just showing up. I try to take Woody one better and add that 99% of success is showing up, taking an active role and doing your best for the cause. If you do this, there is very little chance you will fail.

Perseverance

Perseverance is about sticking to your cause or goal. It means staying with your task over time in an effort to be successful. Perseverance is about persistence, patience and never giving up.

Perseverance is not easy, especially in today's culture. People bounce in and out of causes and often grow tired or disinterested. Once a commitment is made, people are quick to forget, and move on to another newer commitment.

Just looking around our society today we see an assault on our values and institutions. Marriage for example, is an institution where we make vows before God and country that we will stay married "for better or for worse." Regardless of these vows, almost half of all marriages end in divorce.

Contracts, too, are more easily broken today. There was a time when one's word or handshake was a bond. Today, even legal documents and contracts are broken or ignored as people move about in their fickle way. This is rampant in the sports world, where athletes regularly seek to go to another team for more money than they earlier promised to play for.

Even the buildings and constructs of our world today have given in to a "throwaway" mentality. In my own city of Pittsburgh, we recently built two new sports stadiums. The former stadium, Three Rivers Stadium, was only thirty years old, and in good shape as stadiums go, but it gave way to the wrecking ball. Once we find something new, we easily move to end or destroy that which we have known.

Not long ago, people looked for endurance and longevity in a product or person. Today these elements are not as important. Take automobiles as an example. People would buy and then take good care of their purchase, hoping to get as many years out of it as possible. Now, leasing is the big thing and folks look to upgrade every three years. This throwaway approach has affected even our large purchases.

All of this underscores the very challenging nature of perseverance. If we cannot stay committed to something personal like our marriage, what are the chances of staying committed to a social cause like civil rights or human rights? As younger people enter our culture with less of a commitment to longevity, keeping people vested in change will be that much more difficult. So as we think about perseverance, we must find ways to keep people invested. What does it take to enlist people for the long haul?

Personal Relevance

People must see a personal connection to the cause. This can be done through visioning, or finding a bond and then stressing the linkage to others. Reverend Martin Niemoller, a German clergyman at the time of the Holocaust, offered a powerful example of the ways people are linked together. To challenge the aspects of racism, Niemoller is reported to have said, *"First they came for the socialists, and I did not speak out–because I was not a socialist. Then they came for the trade unionists, and I did not speak out–because I was not a trade unionist. Then they came for the Jews, and I did not speak out–because I was not a Jew. Then they came for me–and there was no one left to speak for me."*

This short verse speaks volumes in how it links people together. Having people find the relationship between the cause and their own personal betterment is a key to personal relevance.

Viable Use of Time

People are most passionate when they feel a connection to the cause, but if they come to find their time wasted or misused, their passion wanes quickly. People must find satisfaction in their work. This notion of time well spent is something I think about often in my work. Usually the key resources at UCP are the volunteers who guide our organization and work freely for our cause. Knowing how valuable time is, I am always evaluating the tasks we ask our volunteers to perform and their satisfaction. If our volunteers do not feel a sense of satisfaction, they will soon drop off from our cause.

What brings satisfaction may vary from person to person, and it is up to the leader to find these "hot" spots and then use them effectively. When I was president of my children's school's parent association I tried to find what motivated our volunteers and developed a framework for this "itch to be scratched." Early on I discovered that some people found excitement in raising money, others in educational aspects, still others in social issues and a last group in community issues. I developed four focused committees and four major goals for my administration that corresponded to each of the areas.

It is important to link people to tasks that are commensurate with their abilities. This means getting to know people and the things they bring to the table. This also means keeping people invested and making sure they know that the contribution they bring to the cause is vital to the overall success.

Rituals and Celebration

A third notion to perseverance relates to the fact that human beings are creatures of habits, and rituals provide the basis for our habits. These rituals make people feel at home and become more committed to their cause. Although we looked at rituals earlier, more needs to be said about this important variable.

Stop and think about anything you hold dear and feel a sense of commitment to and you will be sure to find rituals that surround that cause. Churches and religious celebrations are wrought with rituals that you can count on and look forward to. Rituals carried out by the family anchor perseverance to family issues. Even simple social rituals that hold people together offer a clue to the challenge of perseverance.

Celebration, too, is a type of ritual that is critical to long-term commitment. Celebrations almost always include food and drink and are designed to reframe and refresh people. Celebrations also can include music and song that bond and energize people.

A number of years ago I spent some time at the Highlander Center for Social Change. One clear lesson to me was the importance of music and song to the gathering. Each night, after dinner, we would sit together and sing, each person selecting a song. Many songs were inspirational, or were religious hymns; some were not. Regardless, the energy generated by the singing created deep impressions that I can vividly recall today, many years later. There is magic in music.

Identifying People

One final thing that is sure to focus people on the cause is when the leader remembers their names. When people are remembered and acknowledged, strong bonds can be created. Getting to know people's names is one of the great precursors to life success. People have written bestselling business books based on the premise of memory of names.

Payoff

If all of the steps in this framework are followed, it seems that some success should occur. It might not lead to full cultural shifting, but positive aspects should be realized. This notion of payoff can be the ultimate jewel in the crown of change. Payoff is often not the end, but just the beginning. As the goal is obtained, the change will not be long-standing if it is not anchored in the culture. Thus, all the notions of cultural shifting become critical in the payoff stage to keep the new innovation vital in the culture.

As such, an understanding of change must be accompanied by the personal elements so critical to managing the change process. To talk about change without an exploration of leadership is like talking about the music of Paul Simon without acknowledging the poetic influence of Art Garfunkel. Each can stand alone, but together they produce magic. So let us turn next to explore the dynamic aspects of leadership.

NO GREAT IMPROVEMENT IN THE LOT OF MANKIND IS POSSIBLE UNTIL A GREAT CHANGE TAKES PLACE IN THE FUNDAMENTAL CONSTITUTION OF THEIR MODES OF THOUGHT.

— J. S. MILLS

*LEADERSHIP IS THE ABILITY TO STEP OUTSIDE THE CULTURE THAT CRE-
ATED THE LEADER AND START EVOLUTIONARY CHANGE PROCESSES THAT
ARE MORE ADAPTIVE.*

— E. SCHEIN

CHAPTER 6
Cultural Leadership

A look at any major change effort can be tracked back to those who offered formal and informal leadership to the cause. In the disability rights movement, for example, the tracks of leadership can be traced to the mid-1950s and a man named Ed Roberts. At the time, Ed Roberts was a student at the University of California by day, but a nursing home resident at night, tethered to an iron lung due to his polio. Much like his contemporaries in the civil rights movement, Roberts experienced the life of a second-class citizen by being treated as a medical entity. Using lessons from the civil rights movement, Roberts started the "independent living movement" and opened up a new world for millions of Americans with disabilities.

Yet Roberts was not alone. His vision for equality was fueled by other disability rights advocates, the creation of organizations dedicated to empowerment and equality and to many informal leaders who offered support and assistance along the way. Following Roberts have been people like Evan Kemp, Justin Dart and others who have continued the movement. These and other leaders have spawned various groups that continue the cause for disability rights. Today we have organizations such as the National Organization on Disability (NOD), the Association for Persons in Supported Employment (APSE), The Association for Persons with Severe Handicaps (TASH) and Americans Disabled for Attendant Programs Today (ADAPT).

This blending of people and groups has always been a key element in leading any major change. Martin Luther King had the Southern Christian Leadership Organization, Gloria Steinem had the National Organization of Women and Roberts had the Centers for Independent Living. These, and countless other examples, had official and unofficial leaders playing a role in the cause. Thus, any discussion on change immediately leads to an exploration of leadership. So often the vision or goal for an organization or group is either driven or supported by the official or unofficial leader of the organization. Clearly if we want to understand change and cultural shifting, we need to think about leadership.

First, leadership can be official, as in formally elected or selected people who play an executive, president or CEO role. These individuals are already empowered to speak for the organization and to set the tone. Most important to the tone is to develop a vision and goal for the group.

Leaders might not necessarily be formal, but also can include those who have informal or native power within an organization. These are the individuals who are not titled as leaders, but greatly influence the flow of the organization. Either way, leaders can pay attention to the need for vision and promote it within their organizations, or they can ignore the importance of vision and let the organizations drift.

Whether they are official or unofficial, leaders are responsible for change. Consequently, it is prudent to think about notions of leadership and explore elements that might help in the change process. This chapter looks at the elements of leadership and how they can be utilized to drive positive change.

Leadership Profile

Certainly volumes have been written about leadership, and today, any business CEO who has been successful has authored a book on the topic. Si Kahn, noted community organizer, in his book *Organizing* (1982) makes some interesting comments about leaders and offers key leadership qualities. He states that a good leader has at least twenty traits, including: likes people, is a good listener, makes friends easily, builds trust easily, talks well and helps people believe in themselves. A good leader can let others take the credit, works hard and doesn't get discouraged too often. When we think of individual as well as organizational change, these qualities apply to the change process. Of course, qualities alone will not bring the basic change you want, but they sure can help.

Another expert on change, John Kotter (1996), suggests the following mental habits as critical to leadership and change:

1. Risk taking: Willingness to push oneself out of comfort zones.
2. Humble self-reflection: Honest assessment of successes and failures, especially the latter.
3. Solicitation of opinions: Aggressive collection of information and ideas from others.
4. Careful listening: Propensity to listen to others.
5. Openness to new ideas: Willingness to view life with an open mind (p. 183).

These aspects, as identified by Kotter, continue to promote the elements necessary to setting a viable vision. Certainly the notions that each of these elements explores cause us to closely examine our frameworks in an effort to consider a different vision.

Another theorist, Donald Krause, writing in his book *The Way of the Leader* (1997), states:

"Leadership can be defined as the will to control events, the understanding to chart a course, and the power to get a job done, cooperatively using the skills and abilities of other people…The power to lead is…a function of character, not an accident of birth or a prerogative of position." (pp. 3-4)

Another perspective comes from Marshall Sashkin (1992) when he explores the notion of "visionary leadership." This approach suggests three major aspects to visionary leadership. First is the construction of the vision itself. This deals with the creation and enculturation of the vision. Next comes the process of defining an organizational philosophy that focuses the vision and ties organizational programs and policies to the vision. The final aspect centers on the behaviors and practices of the leaders themselves as they attempt to support the vision.

All of these elements are key for the role of the leader in the process of cultural shifting. More than anyone else, leaders, be they change agents or gatekeepers, must understand and embody the elements of leadership and vision to see change through.

Leadership Framework

Cultural shifting is a process that must be led, and major change does not happen by chance. We have discovered in previous chapters that a change agent or gatekeeper is often the start point for change. This innovative person usually conceives the idea for a new way. Next, however, more positive gatekeepers must be enlisted to begin to legitimatize the new way and call others to join them. As more and more people join the cause, a cultural shift happens. All of this is due to the insights of the change agent or leader. To better understand the role and action of the change agent we must understand leadership frameworks.

Here is a framework I prepared a few years ago for a seminar on leadership I led at a trade association retreat. Knowing that the audience would be seasoned administrators, I pondered for weeks how I might couch this notion of leadership and change. Then one morning, as insights often unfold, the notion of a leadership framework fell into place. Much like the SPARKLE approach explored in the last section, I decided to use a mnemonic structure to drive home the points: the seven Vs of leadership. I believe that leadership and change flows as follows:

Values • Vision • Venue • Verification • Variability • Veracity • Victory

---

Values

It is not too lofty to state that the road to leadership must start with a solid understanding and focus on values. Values can be defined as the beliefs and attitudes we hold dear. They refer to the things we care about and strive for in our lives. Our values are the key tenets that guide our lives and our organizations. They are the things that we will not compromise.

Many of us have not taken a good stock of our values. In fact, I wonder if you have ever sat down and itemized the things that you feel represent your values. Most people I know have not. And if you did, what would they be? What do you feel are the sacrosanct things you believe about life? What do you think are the sacrosanct values of business?

A few years back, the organization I work for in Pittsburgh did just this. We explored our values and identified a thorough list of things that we hold dear. We included all the key stakeholders of our agency to assure that there was a flow of values throughout our organization and that we were not making any assumptions. The key items we identified were:

- We recognize that all people share the same basic human needs.
- We recognize the innate value and dignity of all people.
- We promote informed choice.
- We promote inclusion of all people.
- We do not hurt people.

Organizations, like people, must have values that drive the programs and services offered. Values are the foundation of the development of programs. Unless they are strong, maintained and regularly strengthened, all elements of the organization are weakened. We must know our personal values and work to have these developed into organizational values. Then we must work diligently to keep them strong. Yet most organizations assume that their values are fine. They defer the time and attention needed for values and apply this energy in programs or fundraising. This could lead to serious mistakes.

The organizational leader is responsible for the development, health and maintenance of the organizational values. As a good steward, he or she must assure that the values are reviewed and people have the opportunity to recommit to them. Stakeholders of an organization cannot hear enough about the values.

Vision

Vision is the interpretation of the values into the organization's mission or action statement. That is, vision is the ability to articulate values in a relatively clear and concise way. An interesting exercise on vision is to gather some key stakeholders of your organization and ask them to draw or interpret your organization in a picture. If you did this, what would your organization look like? How would you illustrate the values of your agency or company?

Jenny Craig, the weight reduction organization, knows the value of visioning. Jenny Craig often advertises by posting billboards that show a before-after picture. The before side displays a person, often frowning and clearly overweight. The after side shows a photo of the same person, now lean and smiling. This juxtaposition is more than an effective advertisement, it is an illustration of the power of visioning. Here you see, side-by-side, a vision of what is, and more importantly, what could be, if you sign on with Jenny Craig. You can vision the future.

Venue

Venue is a word that refers to a setting. It identifies the elements that build the environment in which something is to happen. By considering the venue, we are acknowledging the current setting in which we operate. Venue also refers to the culture, the key points of influence and the impact of these influences. All venues or cultures have some key ingredients that can be identified in order to successfully navigate through them. These ingredients have been outlined earlier in this book, but for those reading selectively they are:

- *Rituals*–the deeply etched behaviors that are practiced by all players in the venue. These rituals are ones that are not debated or challenged. Everyone subscribes to the rituals.
- *Patterns*–the social distance and physical behaviors of the players of the culture. These patterns are observable and in many ways display the hierarchy of the culture.
- *Jargon*–the words and phrases used by members of the venue to communicate. They represent the specific aspects of the venue and help players navigate through the culture.
- *Memory*–the history and background of the venue. Usually found in photos and stories, the memory anchors the culture and gives the players something to work toward.

For a leader, understanding the venue is critical to success. Indeed, the major drive for leadership is to influence the venue to display the values that are considered vital to success.

Another aspect is to consider the broader notion of the outside influences that affect the venue. For most of us, this would be the broader paradigm of our industry. For example, if you work in a human services venue, then the outside influences of government and funding sources would be a critical ingredient for consideration. Given that my practice for leadership and change is in human services, current notions of conservatism and cynicism become important for me to consider. These notions certainly will influence how my venue processes information and impact the reality of the vision we have designed.

Other aspects of the venue relate closely to the times we are in. For example, the information explosion of computers and the Internet has created an overload for most people. The easy availability of information makes competition for attention all the greater. The pace of information has rippled to the greater society as well. Look around and you see people on the go at almost nonstop speed. Running here and there, people are looking for the quick fix and instant gratification. Even waiting in line for fast food can lead to stressed-out looks on the faces of customers. I recently overheard a person behind me in a McDonald's line complain that the two-minute wait she was experiencing was not her idea of fast food.

This fast-paced reality cuts a number of ways. On the one hand it promotes a sense of the quick fix. If things do not happen instantaneously, then we are annoyed. This need for an immediate solution can override the reality of some of the natural complexities of life. Another concern is that it also promotes an intolerance and contempt for things and people who are slow by design. This intolerance can play out in a number of ways, but generally the end result is negative.

Verification

At this stage, attention turns to consistency of actions to the vision. Do your actions reflect the beliefs and values purported by the organization? That is, if you say you believe in listening to your customers, do your actions reflect this belief? What evidence do you have that it does? Are you looking to verify and evaluate your values?

Verification is the process by which you come to know whether you do what you believe. To verify, however, requires that the leader is present and in touch with the day-to-day interactions of his or her team. To do this, leadership gurus such as Tom Peters suggest we walk around our organizations or take a close view of our lives and catch ourselves or others doing things "right." Other methods are to invite outside "eyes" such as accreditation or evaluation teams to monitor or look at our services or actions. Regardless of approach, we must not be fooled into thinking that the mere presence of services or actions is tantamount to values truly being in place.

Max DePree recommended one interesting method that can help in the verification process in his book, *Leadership Is an Art* (1989). DePree suggests that the organization cultivate "roving philosophers" who are passionate about the values and capable of promoting conversations about them. DePree feels that if people stay conscious about the values, they also will remain vigilant to them. Along with keeping people vigilant, the philosophers can be helpful in verifying the extent to which the values are present in the everyday operations of the organization.

Variability

Variability refers to flexibility, and any organization in today's venue must be flexible to survive. Indeed, even individual change mandates a strong sense of variability. The notion of flexibility is best understood in a willingness to be open. The successful organization or person is an open one accessible to ideas, recommendations and feedback. Of course, an openness to change is based upon all the elements previously discussed.

One way of keeping variable is to listen closely to the philosophers in your organization or in your life. These people can impart wisdom. One can listen best, however, when one is ready to listen. Trained counselors know that listening is an art, and leaders do well to pay attention to ways of listening better. Some ideas are:

Suspend your judgments–As leaders we all have thoughts and opinions on the elements of our work. We must work hard to hold these thoughts down so as to give a viable chance to really hear those around us. This is especially true if these people have critical things to say. Our tendency is to immediately judge the person delivering the message rather than listen closely to the message itself.

Prepare to listen–Our days are often fast-paced and we have much to do. When people approach us to share some thoughts, we have to prepare to hear them. This means we must make the time to remove the distractions that often get in the way. We have to be ready to hear what people are saying to us.

Attend–To attend is to give attention to the person who is sharing with you. Attending is best done when people attempt to even out the communication process by sitting across from one another, leaning forward and establishing eye contact. We can hold our calls, shut the door and focus on what the person is saying.

Another key element of variability is to seek out information from other paradigms. Often we are so inundated with the information from our own mental model that we do not get a chance to explore things from other arenas. A leader willing to change seeks out alternative material.

A typical trap that often harnesses an organization's or person's ability to be variable is when policies, procedures or plans lock you in. The scientific approach of understanding and trying to predict and control all variables can be a deterrent to change. Of course we must have some basic structure, but to become a slave to our own regulations can be devastating. Leaders need to walk a tightrope on this vital issue. You want to predict enough to not set yourself up for failure, but you want to also stay open to new and unpredictable things.

Closely tied to this is the organization's ongoing framework for change. Many organizations try to build in some formal insurance for change. Things like board rotation, updates on strategic plans and organizational annual reports are all methodologies that, when used correctly, can help promote variability.

Veracity

Keeping focused on the values, vision and mission of the organization is what is meant by veracity. Most of us face great challenges. The compromising venue can make each day a struggle. Yet any important cause is never had easily. Indeed, all the vital causes that have occurred in recent times could not have happened without veracity as a linchpin.

Yet, how can we be sure to stay the course? How can we keep people enthused and willing to give it their all? Ways to stay vigilant include:

Reflect–Think about what you are trying to do and take inventory on your progress. Try to truly see the forest for the trees.

Celebrate–Make sure that people have the opportunity to pause and celebrate the small victories along the way. Publicly acknowledge and praise individuals who are "walking the walk."

Play–The power of humor and play can go a long way in keeping an organization full of veracity. Make time to assure that your organization is a fun place to work at or visit.

Nurture–Often, in the tougher moments, people are going to get bruised and pushed around a bit. These are the times for leaders to hold on to people and keep them up. Nurturing can happen in a number of ways but the bottom line is to be there with people when the harder times occur.

Victory

If all of these themes are considered and affirmed, organizations (and individuals) will succeed in their mission. This may not mean actually achieving the vision, but certainly steering the organization closer and closer to that goal.

Gandhi said that full effort is full victory. The mere fact that you think through and thoughtfully position yourself or your company in a way that embraces these ideas puts you that much further ahead of your competition. This framework can be helpful because it raises our consciousness to the steps and stages of leadership. The content for the steps is not novel, but the ability to remember and stay on course during the leadership process always can be enhanced.

Even with this or any framework, another key aspect to leadership success in cultural shifting relates to the way we think. This may sound odd, but leadership thinking calls for the leader to guide the thinking of the team to a new place. Like most other aspects of leadership, this is not easy. There are, however, some elements to consider with leadership thinking. Let's turn now to look at them.

Leadership Thinking

If we are confronted with change, or are forced to have to do something new or want to push ourselves ahead of the curve, we must examine the cognitive process and how it allows us to move from point A to point B. Thinking, or cognition, is the way we assemble the ideas and concepts in our minds to engage with our world. How people think greatly affects cultural shifting.

Thinking is often seen as the precursor to learning. Before we can learn, we must be able to think. To think is to study, amass information and critically construct the information into a framework that makes sense. Indeed, the Chinese use two characters to identify the word "learning." The first character means "to study" and blends the notion of a child in a doorway attempting to accumulate knowledge. The other character means "to practice constantly." This means one needs to think constantly about a topic if one wants to learn it well.

A key element that has an effect on the notion of thinking is related to self-image and self-concept. Clearly, the basic personality of the thinker sets the tone for how he or she will understand an issue. If someone has a negative perspective on life, his or her major thinking framework will be cautious and suspicious. Conversely, if the person comes from a more positive place, they will orient from an optimistic point of view. The basic perspective of people will drive how they view, think and then act on an issue. As individuals interested in change and action, this should be important information for us to consider.

I was excited to come across the work of Edward de Bono a number of years ago. His work in cognition is well known and respected, but perhaps his greatest contribution has been to introduce the six thinking hats. In *Six Thinking Hats* (1985), de Bono creates an easy and useful cognitive framework to problem-solving and managing change. It is well worth some review here.

De Bono postulates, and most cognitive theorists agree, that people come at the notion of thinking from a core perspective that affects how that same person assembles information to solve problems. This core perspective is a mental model that influences the flow of the thinking process. De Bono has identified six core perspectives and focused them within the context of a color. He uses the colors to help teams (collections of thinkers) to stay on track as they manage a problem. The use of colors helps people to remember the perspective. The theory is that most of us orient from one of these six perspectives. They are:

- *White*–neutral and objective, concerned with facts and figures
- *Red*–emotional or feeling
- *Black*–careful and cautious, the devil's advocate
- *Yellow*–sunny and optimistic
- *Green*–creative, innovative or growth-oriented
- *Blue*–cool and organized, controlled

If you pause to consider your situation, probably one of these perspectives best describes you. This doesn't imply that you cannot use or relate to another perspective, but that your basic orientation starts with your dominant cognitive approach. The key for leadership is to know that solid progress must be balanced around all six perspectives. That is, if your dominant approach is to come from the red perspective, you must be aware that emotions alone cannot be the way to proceed. Again, this does not mean that your gut instinct is bad, only that it must be balanced. Consequently, the six thinking styles offer a framework for leadership or change-oriented thinking. By knowing your start point, you begin to identify the other thinking styles that are necessary for a balanced approach to a problem.

De Bono suggests that organizations or teams apply the process by using the metaphor of hats. In his thesis, the team uses the notion of putting on the appropriate hat to process the issue at hand from that perspective. For example, if the team wants to explore new ideas, all members are asked to wear their green hats. No one is to criticize (black hat) or offer a feeling (red hat) on the idea while the green hats are on. At a later point, the black or red hats may be worn, but the key is for everyone on the team to wear the same hat at the same time to move the idea or issue forward. This unanimity is critical because at any given time, an idea or issue might be stunted by contradictory thinking perspectives offered by others at the same time. We all know the experience of a good idea being driven down by the naysayers. Using the hats and keeping everyone on the same page attempts to prevent this from happening.

As I used de Bono's approach with my own team, I found it to be extremely helpful. We have all six types of thinkers on our team and by harnessing the thinking, we have become more successful. That is because all six perspectives are useful in solving problems or promoting change. But when they are occurring at the same time, they can be destructive.

When we consider individual efforts for changing or problem solving, the notion of six thinking styles becomes more difficult to actualize. With a team, you can move together through the styles, and usually you have a dominant player to push each style. When you are on your own, you continue to be dominated by your own style and often have difficulty bringing another perspective into your analysis. This is natural, as we tend to lean toward that which we know or do best. Unlike the team, which has diversity in styles, the individual must find other ways to bring perspectives that are not natural to them to the fore.

To do this we must find ways to identify and then respect styles or opinions that go against our natural grain. This first requires an awareness of the different styles and then the developing of a habit to use them. Some ideas about doing this are:

- Write down a simple overview of the six styles and keep them in your vision.
- Consider ways that you can advance the non-dominant issues into your approach.
- Find other people in your life who orient from another perspective and ask them to help you analyze problems or issues.
- Consider trigger questions that promote non-dominant approaches.

This concept of a dominant approach to our thinking cannot be overstated. If we orient from a yellow perspective, one of being sunny and optimistic, we might be totally oblivious to the negative, or emotional, consequences of our actions. To the extent possible, we must come to know and acknowledge how we see the world and then balance our actions with input and involvement from the other perspectives. This is much easier said than done.

So, leadership is dependent on thinking. This, in turn, is the raw material of cultural shifting. If we are to promote new ideas, products or people to continue the development of culture, we must deliberately think about the ways this can happen. Leadership thinking helps us with this process.

Now that we have looked at some profiles, frameworks and cognitive aspects, we can turn attention to the last leadership element, that of communication. Without question, the most basic ingredient for cultural shifting is the ability to communicate a new way to the gatekeepers and others willing to embrace something novel. Communication offers a key to change.

Communication and Leadership

"Communication is the problem and the answer" is a line from a popular rock song. This phrase frames the concept very well. Communication is the basis to success or to failure. If I show you a failed organization or relationship, you can usually trace the failure to communication. Equally, find a community or setting that is vibrant and growth-oriented, and you will discover a group that communicates well.

This potency so intrigued me that I chose to do my doctoral work in the area of communication effectiveness. Clearly, if we are going to promote change, shift the culture or make something new happen, we must be able to effectively or even "seductively" communicate.

Communication is a process by which people send and receive messages. Communication effectiveness is to do so in such a manner that a close approximation exists between the message sent and the message received. It requires the manipulation of the process to enhance the potential for communication success. Communication seduction is to use methods or methodologies to lure the receiver into wanting to know or understand more about the message sent.

In the process of communication there are two entities, each with unique spheres of experience coming together in some element of commonality. This implies that the communicator has two major frameworks to initiate the communication. The first is the known element of commonality. If two people find themselves in a class together, the first known element is that both individuals have chosen to take the class. The features of this known element are the class name, reputation, instructor and topic matter. All of these things offer initial fodder for communication.

The second framework is that of assumptions people may make of each other. People have spheres of experience that is a compilation of all the things that have happened to them: family history, education, life experiences and the like. These aspects are not fully known, but assumptions can be made. This is done with direct observation and opportunities to check the accuracy of assumptions through initial communication.

By using both of these frameworks, the known commonality and the assumptions of the individuals' experiences, the communicator will code a message that he or she hopes will be understood and decoded most effectively. At this point of the process—the coding—the message gets constructed with words, gestures and affect and then delivered. The actual decision about which words to use, the specific gestures to apply and the affect to incorporate are made based on the two frameworks. As the message gets sent, it is hoped that it will be decoded and understood and a relay message that builds on the first message will occur.

While this sounds sterile as we discuss it in this context, the process happens so quickly that often we do not think through all the ways we could enhance or "seductively" construct the message so it is likely to be heard and understood. Consequently, the process of communication falls prey to so many distractions and distortions that the net result is that most communication is not effective. In fact, in many situations, it is amazing that things get communicated at all.

Using these frameworks in a thoughtful way will begin to enhance the communication, but research has shown that adding the dimension of "expressive affect" will ratchet up the effectiveness to a seductive level. Since the early 1970s, researchers have manipulated a number of variables to find ways to enhance the communication process. Most of this research was kicked off by a social scientist by the name of John Ware. His work was spurred by a study he conducted in 1975 and was published in both academic as well as popular journals as the "Dr. Fox Effect."

Fascinated by the notion of communication effectiveness, Ware conducted a study at the University of Illinois. He hired an actor, wrote a nonsense script, invented a bogus Dr. Fox complete with an impressive biography and then invited local social workers, counselors, teachers and psychologists to a contrived lecture. He prepped Dr. Fox, who practiced an expressive approach to the script, and then he carried out the study. Close to one hundred professionals came to the free lecture sponsored by the University of Illinois. Dr. Fox spoke on the topic of "mathematical game theory and behavior" for an hour, answered questions and then left the stage to rousing applause. John Ware then did an exit evaluation of the lecture with basic questions about Dr. Fox. He asked if the audience had heard of him, read his books and found his theories useful.

As it turned out, the majority of the members of the audience loved Dr. Fox. Some of them claimed they had heard of him, a few said they had read his books and the majority said that they thought his theories were useful. Yet, for all of this acclaim, the lecture was nonsense! This so amazed John Ware that he coined the term "Dr. Fox Effect" and began the exploration of a body of knowledge now known as "educational seduction."

For people interested in change, the concept of educational seduction is useful. Cultural shifting is about influence and action. Ware articulated what many generations had known, that some people could so influence others with seductive communication that they could get those same people to do positive or negative things. Adolf Hitler, Charles Manson and Jimmy Jones, among others, had the seductive ability to influence followers to do cruel and harmful things.

My interest in this concept was for just the opposite. Ware proved and history acknowledged that some people could seduce others to do wrong or negative things, but we also know there have been many people who have used the gift of communication seduction to promote positive and valuable things. I was intrigued about how seductive communication could be used by change agents or gatekeepers to promote new people, ideas or products within the context of the community. Given the goals of the change agent, or the natural influence of the gatekeeper, if this could be coupled with educational seduction theory, amazing things might happen.

To test this approach, I conducted an experiment similar to Ware's, but instead of nonsense content, I inserted viable and useful information. To further test the difference between styles, I manipulated two distinct communication approaches, but kept the content positive and viable. I hired an actor and had him learn the content for a college class lecture. He delivered the lecture to two similar classes, but in two distinct styles—direct and expressive. The direct style was focused, but very businesslike. The actor stayed mostly at the podium and used a serious and direct affect. The expressive style had the actor moving much more and inserting vocal inflection and gestures. My study verified what Ware had initiated. The expressive communication style had a greater impact on the audiences I researched. So in the notion of change and communication, effectiveness becomes an important and useful concept. The more we can engage the audience we are attempting to influence, the easier the cultural shift.

▲

Thus leadership, be it from the change agent or gatekeeper, is a process that must be analyzed and understood. Given the pace and energy of our world today, any advantage for the leader is critical. If we are to lead change and become more effective gatekeepers, the component parts of leadership explored in this chapter become essential.

THE SIGNIFICANT PROBLEMS WE FACE TODAY CANNOT BE SOLVED AT THE SAME LEVEL WE WERE AT WHEN WE CREATED THEM.
— ALBERT EINSTEIN

THE FIRST STEP IN THE EVOLUTION OF ETHICS IS A SENSE OF SOLIDAR-
ITY WITH OTHER HUMAN BEINGS.

—ALBERT SCHWEITZER

CHAPTER 7
Strategies for Cultural Shifting

To understand the notions of community and cultural shifting is one thing, but to take advantage of and leverage them is quite another. As advocates, we need to take the theories identified in this book and turn them into action. Change is about blending reflection and action. It revolves around thinking about things and having this thinking influence our behavior. Certainly the process of change is challenging. Just when we have some things understood, a new approach seems to emerge to push us down a new lane. Whatever field you are in, the elements explored in this book should have some relevance.

All of the elements that we have looked at apply to agency change as well as to any other type of change. Regardless of your position within your place of employment, some of the strategies covered can be of help. If we know that positive gatekeepers are an essential ingredient to cultural shifting, how can we come to find them, or more importantly, become one? This is no easy task, but there clearly are things we can learn and attempt to adopt. If we stay alert to these notions we can more easily spot potential gatekeepers. We also can keep our consciousness high so we can remember to practice these very same things in our own lives. Let's discuss some strategies.

Be Positive

Since the positive gatekeeper is the single most critical element to building community, learning how to identify, promote or become a gatekeeper becomes a key part of community building and cultural shifting. We know that positive gatekeepers tend to be positive people. That is, they are people who smile, reach out and see the new person, idea or product as being useful or helpful to the community, despite any differences.

This positive approach cannot be stressed enough. Positive people are more attractive than negative people. Although this is conventional wisdom, most of us still struggle with a strong tendency to be negative. Following "Pareto's Principle" where 20% of the community who tend to be negative will greatly influence the 80% who tend to be positive or neutral, we have a subconscious drive to think about the bad around us. If we want to be positive gatekeepers, we must remind ourselves of that which is good. By looking for the good, we set the tone for capacities and solution-oriented activity.

So how do we try to remain positive about life? With all due respect to the multitude of books and essays on this subject, it seems to me that the most basic element for positive thinking is to remain conscious about the importance of positive attitudes. If we can just remember to think about the positive elements of life, we have at least a chance to keep positive in our actions.

Thus, if we are looking for positive gatekeepers to influence culture, or if we want to be a positive gatekeeper for our own world, the first critical act is to THINK about it! Know what you are looking for, or what you want to be. Remind yourself of cultural shifting agenda and you are more apt to obtain it.

The next time you are out in the community, look closely around the room and see if you can pick out the positive people. This is better done in a setting where you do not know the other people well, as the biases of familiarity might color your perspective. Notice who smiles more, or who seems to be more open in posture and action. See if you can pick out those who are dressed in a more positive way. Watch closely their behaviors with others. Do they listen as much as they talk? Do they demonstrate a genuine interest in the people they are with? Do they seem alive and alert?

Then, after you have identified the positive person, if you have the courage, introduce yourself. Let the person know that you are a student of cultural shifting and that you are doing fieldwork on the positive gatekeeper, and you identified him or her as a positive person. The person may think you're crazy, but will be flattered. Who knows, you might just make a new friend in the bargain.

Reach Out

Positive gatekeepers reach out to others. They are friendly, introduce themselves in new situations and cater to others. This reaching out is evident when you look at the basic behaviors of positive gatekeepers. They care about others and show this in their actions. This reaching out manifests in smiles, eye contact, handshakes or other physical gestures of inclusion.

If you are looking to find a positive gatekeeper in a new group, either for yourself or for someone you are helping to become included, it is critical to observe basic group interactions. Again, notice who reaches out, who says hello, who waves or who shows welcome to other members. This person is probably a positive gatekeeper in the group. Similarly, if you want to be a positive gatekeeper, then do the same – reach out to others. Introduce yourself, say hello first, extend a hand to others. These simple actions are the ones that lead to inclusion and set the tone for cultural shifting. Indeed the best way to identify these elements is to practice doing them.

If you are looking for or want to be a positive gatekeeper, then pay attention to the concept of hospitality. In my earlier work, I identified the notion of hospitality as one of the keys to inclusion. Hospitality is about welcoming people, friendships, openness to guests, receptivity to new ideas, generosity and cordiality. There is no question that hospitality is a key variable for the positive gatekeepers.

Take Risks

To embrace new things in a group takes a sense of risk. If the new person, product or idea is not accepted or is threatening to a group, the gatekeeper is at risk of being devalued as well. That is why another element of positive gatekeepers is taking risks. This is not easy to do. Most people prefer to take safe routes in life. Many wait until things are proven or accepted before they will try or use the new item. Most of us do not want to run the risk of failure. This is why there are so few true entrepreneurs in life.

Still, the early adopter is critical to change happening. Without a risk-taker coming forward to take a chance, very little progress will occur. Great inventors have been great risk-takers. These are people who were not afraid of failure or the devaluation that sometimes accompanies failure. They took chances and at some point these chances paid off. In social discourse, risk-takers are the people who are not worried about what others think or say about their behavior. They look for the good in things, reach out and take risks.

Enthusiasm

If anything creates a positive social infection it is enthusiasm. Enthusiasm is the ability to get excited about issues or events around you. People with a knack for enthusiasm are the ones who not only invite others to the table, but also convince them that they will have a good time when they come. Enthusiasm is a raw energy that begs involvement. It incites others to join in.

Stop and think about the enthusiastic people you know or have met. Regardless of your feelings about their agenda, you had to feel engaged by their energy. Enthusiastic people exude a sense that their cause is the best one and that you should get into the parade.

Sports teams harness the power of enthusiasm. The more people who can join into the cause of the team, the greater the potential success of the team. Basketball programs talk about the sixth player when they refer to the potency of the enthusiastic fans at the arena. The more the coach (or change agent) can build an enthusiastic base, the easier the team will find success.

Being enthusiastic means that you commit to the cause. You believe in what you are doing and you show it in your behavior. You don't have to be the cheerleader, but you need to be consistent in your actions. When your enthusiasm hits a chord with another person's interest in the cause, magic can happen.

These actions, along with other aspects of hospitality, are important if we are looking to become, or find, positive gatekeepers. So, beyond the academic exercise of exploring the elements of cultural shifting, we also must think about the actions necessary to make this shift happen.

Flexibility

To bring about change often requires that the gatekeeper be flexible with his or her cause. Flexibility refers to the ability to give and take as one advances a cause. When we are flexible we are willing to assume some concessions in order to get closer to our ultimate goal. The person who is flexible does not shut themselves off from other possibilities. It might mean giving something to get something.

Successful change agents understand flexibility. They never totally shut down options or other routes to their cause. Although they do not give away the store, they are willing to compromise. People who can do this are always more apt to win simply because there are always bargains in life.

Action-Oriented

To be a gatekeeper means to act on behalf of a person, idea or product. The key to this point is the word act. Without action, new things will never occur. You might talk about it, dream about it, even shout about it, but if you don't act on it, whatever has your passion will not come to be. Action is the critical ingredient of change.

It is amazing to me how passive we have become as a society. Think about your network of friends. How active are they? Do people routinely initiate things, or do they sit back and react, or worse, do nothing! As we move more and more into an information society, people are sitting passively at their computers passing ideas or thoughts. This is not to mean that the passing of ideas is not good. Indeed, the passing or promotion of ideas is an active event, but the backdrop to this might be terribly passive. Sometimes then, this passivity begins to stunt your energy in other ways and before you know it you become lethargic even with your ideas.

The idea of action-orientation is to say that change agents and gatekeepers need to keep active in body, mind and spirit. The more we keep active the easier it is to promote change.

Brevity

One key ingredient that successful change agents and gatekeepers seem to know and apply is brevity. Essentially, brevity is that ability to condense your issue or goal into a concise and succinct framework that is easy for others to understand. Many a good cause has not ignited because other members of the community did not easily understand the goal or direction of the cause. With brevity, the change agent easily can convey the goal and get people engaged in action.

One test of brevity is to think about the goal or issue you are looking to have adopted. If you cannot describe your goal in a few sentences, with no more than two minutes of discussion, then you have not achieved the brevity necessary for successful engagement. Madison Avenue understands the notion of brevity. Consider any commercial you see on TV or read in a magazine. If the advertisement cannot get you to understand the product and why you should buy it in thirty seconds, or sometimes less, then the marketing agency has not done its job.

The reason brevity is critical to change is that there are considerable distractions that compete for people's time. If you cannot get and then keep people's attention on your cause, you will lose them in the bargain. Good change agents practice getting their point across quickly and clearly.

Recently I had an experience where brevity was critical. I was asked to deliver testimony to our county council on a proposed "living wage ordinance" for workers in human services. The ordinance called for front line employees to be given an increased wage and proposed that the council increase the county budget for this purpose. According to council rules, I had only three minutes to make my point, and to keep things on time, the council president had a timer set. If you went overtime, they cut you off in mid-sentence. Needless to say, three minutes is very little time to make such an important request, but I focused my comments and practiced with a timer. As I listened to testimonies before mine, it was amazing how many people could not get their points across in time. Most were stopped without getting to their final points. Given my practice, the testimony I gave went off without a hitch. More importantly, the exercise really pushed me to be brief.

So the next time you are called to make a point, consider the principle of brevity. Be crisp and clear and make your point in two minutes. You probably will not only keep the person's attention, but win your cause as well.

Creativity

In most change activity, the more creative your approach, the more invested your people become. Good change agents and gatekeepers are often creative people. They know how to get people's attention and keep focussed on their idea, product or a new person they are escorting into the culture.

Creativity comes in many ways and in a variety of packages. Stop and think about memorable advertisements you might have seen on TV or in print. The ones you recall are those that struck a creative chord and kept your attention. The more creative something is, the more apt people are to consider it. You can't shift the culture unless you first engage it.

Conclusion

The notion of change and cultural shifting is a multifaceted, dynamic process. It is one that we all are called to consider in our lives, but is easier said than done. It is a process that blends and demands the focus of a number of critical variables. We must appreciate the:

- vexing paradox of wanting more, while fearing change
- important elements of culture and community
- critical role of the gatekeeper
- component parts of the change process
- overarching ingredients of leadership
- essential focus on the communication process
- notions of being positive, flexible, action-oriented and enthusiastic

All of these things give rise to the process of change. They are not complex or overly intellectual. They often unfold without much detailed or even strategic thinking. Sometimes they are not in our consciousness at all, yet positive change might still unfold. In these situations we just may have been inordinately lucky.

The bold face of it is that change is never easy. If we want, need or must change, we have serious work cut out for our organizations or ourselves. This doesn't mean that we will always be successful, but it does suggest that we have a greater possibility for success if we address these issues. This challenge can be reduced greatly if we consider the elements in this book.

At the bottom line, change really boils down to a person doing something differently. He or she steps outside of what was done or known and attempts something new or different. When you reduce change to this simple equation, it doesn't seem so intimidating. It doesn't necessarily make it easier, but it does give us a more hopeful approach.

As we think about that one person doing something new or different, it leads to a starting point for greater change. As others begin to observe that one person doing something new of different, they begin to say, "*So can I.*" These early adopters who follow the gatekeeper begin to further demonstrate the viability of the new or different thing. Then others follow suit. Before you know it, the culture has shifted to embrace the new or different thing initiated by the first person.

Jean Vanier once said, "*How can one understand some things so easily, yet so often fail to put them in play.*" And he is right. In their basic elements, the concepts of culture, community and change are not deep and esoteric. They are, quite simply, the ingredients of life. Yet change remains the greatest of barriers and generates the deepest of fears.

▲

This book was initiated to shine a brighter light on this phenomenon we all face and deal with. Each of the elements explored, by themselves, will not solve the puzzle of change. If they are taken as a whole, however, and applied in a systematic way, the challenge of change becomes more palatable.

As you put this book down, I invite you to consider these notions now in your life. Understand that you are the key to change happening in your life and in your organization. The best way to deal with change is to take it head on. As a gatekeeper you can make anything happen. All you have to do is try!

THERE ARE VICTORIES OF THE SOUL AND SPIRIT. SOMETIMES, EVEN IF YOU LOSE, YOU WIN.

— ELI WIESEL

ONE PERSON WITH A BELIEF IS A SOCIAL POWER EQUAL TO NINETY-NINE WHO HAVE ONLY INTERESTS.

— J. S. MILL

EPILOGUE

As this book comes to a close, I feel it is more than the conclusion of a book, but the sunset of a trilogy that includes *Interdependence, Beyond Difference,* and now *Cultural Shifting.* As you think about changing things in your community, three important variables must be combined. These are:

1. What exists now, and what I want to occur (a new conceptual framework).
2. How I personally feel and relate to this new framework.
3. How I can get others to embrace and adopt the new framework.

In essence, these three variables are the corpus of each of the books of the trilogy. *Interdependence* is about the new framework, *Beyond Difference* is the internal feelings about this framework and *Cultural Shifting* is how we can promote this (or any) new framework. These books address the changes needed in human services, but *Cultural Shifting* is the one that goes beyond human services. Indeed, regardless of the framework you are interested in seeing adopted, I believe this book has something that will work for you.

So as I close out this trilogy I think back to the beginning. It is truly interesting what has changed and what still remains the same in the span of these three books. Consider these world facts in the past ten years.

1990

- George Bush is the 41st President of the United States.
- Nelson Mandela is freed in South Africa.
- Hundreds are killed in a Philippines earthquake.
- Sampras wins the U.S. Open.
- Walesa is elected President of Poland.
- Iraq invades Kuwait.
- The Liberian president is assassinated.
- Pope John Paul II prays for world peace.
- Tensions flare in the Middle East.
- Leonard Bernstein dies.
- CDs are the rage in technology.

1995

- Bill Clinton is the 42nd President of the United States.
- Nelson Mandela is the President of South Africa.
- Hundreds are killed in a Kobe, Japan earthquake.
- Sampras wins Wimbledon.
- Walesa loses the presidency of Poland.
- Turkey invades Iraq.
- The Israeli prime minister is assassinated.
- Pope John Paul II prays for world peace.
- Tensions flare in the Middle East.
- Dean Martin dies.
- PCs are the rage in technology.

2000

- George W. Bush is the 43rd president of the United States.
- Nelson Mandela retires as president of South Africa.
- Hundreds are killed in earthquake in Turkey.
- Sampras wins Wimbledon.
- Walesa loses in bid for president of Poland.
- The Serbian leader is assassinated.
- Pope John Paul II prays for world peace.
- Tensions flare in the Middle East.
- Walter Matthau dies.
- DVDs are the rage in technology.

Things come and go, sometimes lasting, at other times they flash and are gone. New ideas change things as they hit, usually for the better, but not always. World events push things left or right on the political scale. And people come and go, leaving their marks for good or for bad.

Yet there is a constant in all of this. As these people, ideas or products begin to make their mark, different as they may be, the way they influence the culture is a constant. That is, the notions of rituals, patterns, jargon, memory and gatekeepers all remain a constant in how the community embraces new things.

As we close *Cultural Shifting*, think about how change and consistency create a powerful paradox. Human beings are predictable animals with unpredictable ideas, products and influences. To balance this paradox opens a whole new window on the notion of change.

This past decade has been an exciting one for me and for the concept of shifting to a culture of interdependence. I have had the opportunity to visit most every state in the United States and every province in Canada to share ideas. I have met some unbelievable people in the course of this journey. I have watched things come and go, always making way for new things. I have tried to be a good student and purveyor of change. I have tried to share what I have learned and apply it as best I could.

Ending this trilogy now opens a new beginning. Thanks for taking the time to read through this book and the others as well. Please share it with a friend. I plan to continue to explore, write and speak publicly and I hope my journey at some point meets up with yours. As I am always happy to compare notes, I have signed off this epilogue with my mailing addresses and other ways to be in touch. I wish you all the best as you grow and change. Be well in your passage.

Al Condeluci
4638 Centre Ave.
Pittsburgh, PA 15213
412-683-7100, extension 329
acondeluci@aol.com

LIFE IS MADE UP OF SMALL COMINGS AND GOINGS AND FOR EVERYTHING A PERSON TAKES WITH THEM, THERE IS SOMETHING THEY MUST LEAVE BEHIND.

— HERMAN RAUSHER

REFERENCES

Alinsky, Saul. (1960). *Rules for Radicals*. New York: Vantage Press.

American Heritage Dictionary, Third Edition. (1992). New York: Houghton Mifflin Co.

Bennis, Warren. (1999). *Managing People Is like Herding Cats*. Provo, UT: Executive Excellence Publishing.

Block, P. (1987). *The Empowered Manager: Positive Political Skills at Work*. San Francisco: Jossey Bass.

Condeluci, Al. (1991). *Interdependence: The Route to Community*. Boca Raton, FL: CRC Press.

Condeluci, Al. (1996). *Beyond Difference*. Delray Beach, FL: St. Lucie Press.

Conner, Daryl. (1992). *Managing at the Speed of Change*. New York: Villard Books.

Corbin, Carolyn. (September, 14, 1999). Address: *Opening General Session*. Seattle, WA: RSA Region X Conference.

Covey, Steven. (1990). *Seven Habits of Highly Effective People*. New York: Simon and Schuster.

De Bono, Edward. (1985). *Six Thinking Hats*. New York: Little, Brown and Co.

DePree, Max. (1989). *Leadership Is an Art*. New York: Dell Publishing.

Freire, Paulo. (1973). *Education for a Critical Consciousness*. New York: Continuum Press.

Freire, Paulo. (1989). *Pedagogy of the Oppressed*. New York: Continuum Press.

Gatto, John. (1992.) *Dumbing Us Down*. Philadelphia, PA: New Society Publishers.

Gladwell, Malcolm. (2000). *The Tipping Point*. New York: Little, Brown and Co.

Hanifan, L. J. (1916) "The Rural School Community Center." *Annals of the American Academy of Political and Social Science*. 67: 130-138.

Louis Harris and Associates (1998). *1998 N.O.D./Harris Survey of Americans with Disabilities*.

Helmstetter, S. (1986). *What to Say When You Talk to Your Self : The Major New Breakthrough to Managing People, Yourself, and Success*. Grindle Pr Audio

Horton, Miles. (1990). *The Long Haul*. New York: Doubleday.

Hunsaker, Phillip, and Alessandra, Anthony. (1980). *The Art of Managing People*. New York: Simon and Schuster.

Kahn, Si. (1982). *Organizing*. New York: McGraw Hill.

Kotter, John. (1996). *Leading Change*. Boston: Harvard Business School Press.

Krause, Donald. (1997). *The Way of the Leader*. New York: Perigee Books.

Lewin, Kurt. (1958). "Group Decisions and Social Change." *Readings in Social Psychology*. Maccoby, Newcomb and Hartley (Eds.). New York: Holt, Rinehart and Winston.

Lieber, John G., and McConnell, Charles R. (1999). *Management Principles for Health Professionals*. Gaithersburg, MD: Aspen Publications.

Lynch, D. and Kordis, P. (1988) *Dolphin Strategies*. Brain Technologies Corp.

McFarlan, F. Warren. (1999). "Don't Assume the Shoe Fits." *Harvard Business Review* (November-December).

McKnight, John. (1988). *Beyond Community Services*. Evanston, IL: Center of Urban Affairs and Policy Research.

Moore, Stephen. (1995). *Sociology*. Chicago, IL: NTC Publishing.

Nisbit, Robert. (1972). *Quest for Community*. New York: Oxford University Press.

Oakley, Ed, and Krug, Doug. (1994). *Enlightened Leadership*. New York: Fireside Books.

Putnam, Robert. (2000). *Bowling Alone*. New York: Simon and Schuster.

Rosen, Robert. (1996). *Leading People*. New York: Penguin Books.

Sashkin, M. (1992). "Strategic Leadership Competencies: What Are They? How Do They Operate? What Can Be Done to Develop Them?" In R.L. Phillips and J.G. Hunt (Eds.), *Leadership: A Multiorganizational-Level Perspective*. New York: Quorum Books.

Schein, Edgar. (1992). *Organizational Culture and Leadership*. San Francisco: Josey Bass.

Schermerhorn, John R., Hunt, James G., and Osborn, Richard N. (2000). *Organizational Behavior*. New York: John Wiley and Sons.

Senge, Peter. (1990). *The Fifth Discipline*. New York: Doubleday/Currency.

Sussman, Marvin (Ed.). (1959). *Community Structure and Analysis*. New York: Thomas Crowell Co.

Zukav, Gary. (1989). *The Seat of the Soul*. New York: Simon and Schuster.

INDEX

N

need for change in human services 47
negative gatekeepers 30
neighborhood 16

O

organizational change 62
organizational change frameworks 70

P

Pareto's Principle 95
passion 73
patterns of a culture 23
people and change 75
perseverance 80
personal relevance 81
personal zone of change 61
planned change 50
planning process 76
politics 78
position and change 74
positive gatekeepers 29
power triangle 59
pre-baby boomers 54
primary zone of change 61

R

regular points of contact 14
relationships and community 32
resistance to change 53, 63
revolutionary change 59
risk-taking 97
rituals 20
rituals, religious 22
Rosen's Principles for Change 71
routines 22

S

salesmen 30
second order change 57
secondary zone of change 62
segregation 3
self-image 52
sexuality and community 16
six thinking hats 90
social capital 7, 12
social currency 12
social isolation 13
social reciprocity 12
SPARKLE Approach on Leading Change 72
spirituality 15

steps to cultural shifting 37
structural change 58
struggle to improve 8

T

tipping point 55

U

unplanned change 50

V

values 85
variability 88
venue 37, 39, 86
veracity 89
verification 88
vision 86
vision and change 65
vulnerability, human service staff 6

W

work 16

Z

zones of change 60